Frontispiece: Memory and survival in *Trois Couleurs: Bleu*
By kind permission of Artificial Eye

Memory and Survival
The French Cinema of Krzysztof Kieślowski

LEGENDA

LEGENDA, founded in 1995 by the European Humanities Research Centre of the University of Oxford, is now a joint imprint of the Modern Humanities Research Association and Maney Publishing. Titles range from medieval texts to contemporary cinema and form a widely comparative view of the modern humanities, including works on Arabic, Catalan, English, French, German, Greek, Italian, Portuguese, Russian, Spanish, and Yiddish literature. An Editorial Board of distinguished academic specialists works in collaboration with leading scholarly bodies such as the Society for French Studies and the British Comparative Literature Association.

MHRA

The Modern Humanities Research Association (MHRA) encourages and promotes advanced study and research in the field of the modern humanities, especially modern European languages and literature, including English, and also cinema. It also aims to break down the barriers between scholars working in different disciplines and to maintain the unity of humanistic scholarship in the face of increasing specialization. The Association fulfils this purpose primarily through the publication of journals, bibliographies, monographs and other aids to research.

MANEY
publishing

Maney Publishing is one of the few remaining independent British academic publishers. Founded in 1900, the company has offices both in the UK, in Leeds and London, and in North America, in Boston. Since 1945 Maney Publishing has worked closely with learned societies, their editors, authors, and members, in publishing academic books and journals to the highest traditional standards of materials and production.

LEGENDA

RESEARCH MONOGRAPHS IN FRENCH STUDIES

The Research Monographs in French Studies (RMFS) form a separate series within the Legenda programme and are published in association with the Society for French Studies. Individual members of the Society are entitled to purchase all RMFS titles at a discount.

The series seeks to publish the best new work in all areas of the literature, thought, theory, culture, film and language of the French-speaking world. Its distinctiveness lies in the relative brevity of its publications (40,000–50,000 words). As innovation is a priority of the series, volumes should predominantly consist of new material, although, subject to appropriate modification, previously published research may form up to one third of the whole. Proposals may include critical editions as well as critical studies. They should be sent with one or two sample chapters for consideration to Dr Ann Jefferson, New College, Oxford OX1 3BN.

LEGENDA

RESEARCH MONOGRAPHS IN FRENCH STUDIES 7

Memory and Survival
The French Cinema of Krzysztof Kieślowski

❖

EMMA WILSON

LEGENDA

Modern Humanities Research Association and Maney Publishing
Research Monographs in French Studies 7
2000

Published for the Society for French Studies by the
Modern Humanities Research Association and Maney Publishing
1 Carlton House Terrace
London SW1Y 5DB
United Kingdom

LEGENDA is an imprint of the
Modern Humanities Research Association and Maney Publishing

Maney Publishing is the trading name of W. S. Maney & Son Ltd,
whose registered office is at Hudson Road, Leeds LS9 7DL, UK

ISBN 1 900755 27 0
ISSN 1466–8157

First published 2000
Transferred to digital printing 2005

LEGENDA series designed by Cox Design Partnership, Witney, Oxon

Chief Copy-Editor: Genevieve Hawkins
Printed and bound by Antony Rowe Ltd, Eastbourne

CONTENTS

The Railroad Station

My nonarrival in the city of N.
took place on the dot.

You'd been alerted
in my unmailed letter.

You were able not to be there
at the agreed-upon time.

The train pulled up at Platform 3.
A lot of people got out.

My absence joined the throng
as it made its way toward the exit.

Several women rushed
to take my place
in all that rush.

Somebody ran up to one of them.
I didn't know him,
but she recognized him
immediately.

While they kissed
with not our lips,
a suitcase disappeared,
not mine.

The railroad station in the city of N.
passed its exam
in objective existence
with flying colours.

The whole remained in place.
Particulars scurried
along the designated tracks.

Even a rendezvous
took place as planned.

Beyond the reach of our presence.

In the paradise lost
of probability.

Somewhere else.
Somewhere else.
How these little words ring.

WISŁAWA SZYMBORSKA, *View with a Grain of Sand*

FOR MY MOTHER

ACKNOWLEDGEMENTS

This book was written largely in Paris, in a rooftop flat in Belleville.
I would like to thank Julian Jackson for lending this flat to me and for
offering such a good space in which to work. Beyond this my first
debt is to Michael Moriarty: I am extremely grateful to him for his
interest in this project from the start, for his enthusiasm and
encouragement. Jill Forbes has, as ever, offered inspiration, generous
and judicious comment and insight (in particular into connections
between Kieślowski and French national cinema). With her help, this
project is much enhanced. Keith Reader, equally, has been an
invaluable source of advice and expertise. I am very grateful to them
both. I would like to express my thanks too to Jackie Stacey who
edited an article of mine on *Trois Couleurs: Bleu* for *Screen* and whose
acuity and sensitivity offered me new perspectives on Kieślowski. The
University of Cambridge and Corpus Christi College gave grants
which allowed me to complete research on this project. Kareni
Bannister and Graham Nelson at Legenda have been unfailingly
resourceful. It has been a pleasure to work with them both. I am
grateful too to Genevieve Hawkins for her meticulous editorial work.
Sections from the project, in various forms, have been given as papers
at conferences in Cambridge, London, Keele, Lancaster and Morgan-
town, West Virginia. I am grateful to Faber and Faber for permission
to reproduce 'The Railroad Station' from Wisława Szymborska, *View
with a Grain of Sand* (1996) and to Artificial Eye for permission to
reproduce a still from *Trois Couleurs: Bleu* as the frontispiece.

One of my students, Dominique Oliver, died of leukaemia in
March 1999 while working on a dissertation on memory in Proust
and Colette. Conversations with Dominique inevitably enriched my
thoughts on memory and survival. Many other friends and colleagues
have inspired and shared my love of Kieślowski. I am grateful to
Andrew Lockett for first recommending that I should see *Decalogue*.
I am endebted to Dorota Ostrowska for help with translation from

Polish and for rewarding discussion of film. I would also like to offer thanks to Elza Adamowicz, Victoria Best, Malcolm Bowie, Ann Caesar, Sarah Cooper, Peter Collier, Julia Dobson, Johnnie Gratton, Nick Hammond, Susan Hayward, Leslie Hill, Annette Kuhn, Rosemary Lloyd, Geoff Medland, Mark Pryce, Kathryn Robson, Lynsey Russell-Watts, Michael Sheringham, Mick Thurston, Rachel Volloch, Andrew Webber, Elizabeth Wright and students of Paper 125 (Contemporary European Cinema). My partner, Josephine Lloyd, remains sceptical about Kieślowski, but she has been hugely caring and supportive throughout this project. I am very grateful to her. This book is dedicated to my mother, Jacqueline Wilson, whose love, imagination and inspiration have given me so very much.

In Memoriam

Krzysztof Kieślowski died after a second heart attack on 13 March 1996. He had undergone bypass surgery just two days earlier. He had already long publicly announced his intention to give up filmmaking and lead a life in retirement. Details of his funeral on 19 March 1996 were posted on the internet. A casket with Kieślowski's body was made available for public viewing in a church in Warsaw for two hours. Hundreds of people came to pay their respects, bringing many flowers. The Primate of Poland, Cardinal Jozef Glemp, said a short prayer. The funeral mass was celebrated by Fr Jozef Tischner. Music for the mass was composed specially for the occasion by Zbigniew Preisner, and sung by Elżbieta Towarnicka. Kieślowski was later buried in Powązki cemetery, but the burial ceremony was attended only by his family and closest friends. At the funeral mass, we are told, 'the familiar faces of Zbigniew Preisner, Krzysztof Piesiewicz, Juliette Binoche and Irène Jacob were also seen in the crowd'. The scene reads disquietingly like one which might appear in a Kieślowski film.

This is a study of memory and survival. It has taken shape in the aftermath of Kieślowski's filmmaking; its function is both retrospective and commemorative. Kieślowski is a filmmaker who has frequently taken memory itself, and resurrection, as his subject. It seems peculiarly apt, therefore, to look back at his filmmaking, to survey his work, from the closure and conclusion his death has confirmed. Kieślowski's obituaries stress the double loss, at once human and cinematic, his death has wrought. This only highlights the double pattern of memory traces I draw out in his work.

Kieślowski is a director of intimacy and interiority: he has renewed the representation of the human subject and emotion in cinema. His is a cinema of interference and internal reflection, where space and luminous surface offer the finest, most fragile impressions of states of mind and human consciousness. Foremost in these subjective disclosures are relations of the subject to time, memory and personal history. For Kieślowski, identities are temporal: in their temporality lies their ephemerality, their contingency. He creates a cinema of identity in time and motion. It is profoundly a cinema of regret and loss, yet also a cinema of blind chance and fleeting beauty.

For Kieślowski, memory is bound up with image-making. Cinema is a commemorative art and as such it is commemorated in Kieślowski's work. Where memory is subjective and personal for Kieślowski, it is also cinematic. This is thrown further into relief in his French cinema which is primarily my subject here. Kieślowski's French cinema is in part a cinema of artistic exile and of visual self-consciousness. Kieślowski takes his place in French filmmaking through a series of internal references, homages, debts which filter his vision. Filmic allusions exist as so many memory traces, as moments of exchange between director and cinephile viewer. Kieślowski's memory is made our own, is made up of the images of others, in another language and another country.

Throughout this project, with reluctance and a degree of embarrassment, I adopt an auteurist stance to what I call Kieślowski's cinema. This has seemed appropriate in a study concerned with the self-definition, the temporal and national placing of a small corpus of films. Kieślowski is fast proving the progeny of such poetic directors as Bergman and Tarkovsky, and as such now enjoys posthumously a certain degree of adulation. Since the corpus of his work, his spiritual and philosophical concerns, his visual style, are well defined, easily recognizable and, better still, recognizably significant, his status as European *auteur* seems unquestioned. Yet I should stress that my desire here is not directly to confirm this (or challenge it). For me, the repetitions and (in)constancies of Kieślowski's work are interesting primarily in terms of their challenge to the memory and vigilance of the viewer. Continuity becomes an ironic means of measuring divergence. Likewise Kieślowski, as *auteur*, seeks not so much to affirm his subjectivity and first-person stance as to question the distortions and particularities of subjective vision, and of personal cinema. An auteurist approach risks appearing outmoded, completist, erroneously self-assured. Kieślowski's cinema offers no such certainties. In a sense, he frequently takes as his subject the desire for mastery of critic and spectator alike, only to show the fissures and warps in the field of vision. His is a cinema of optical illusion and mental trauma: as such it is a cinema of paradox sustaining itself despite interruption and intrusion. Survival is the surprising subject of his work, survival in denial and disavowal, survival in the present and present absence of the past. Kieślowski's cinema continually re-presents itself. Yet its memory traces are indelible, insistent. It is to their survival in my mind that I owe the impulse to write this work.

I never met Krzysztof Kieślowski. I have only seen fleeting cinematic and photographic images of him. One such image appears in *Rouge* as Kieślowski can be glimpsed briefly amongst the passengers boarding the ferry on the night before the disaster. We see him disappear into the hold amongst the hundreds who will not survive. Here it seems that, in the most unobtrusive manner, Kieślowski creates his own memorial, a barely perceptible *memento mori*.

CHAPTER 1

❖

Images in Crystal
La Double Vie de Véronique

1 Bilingual Film

In his dialogues with Claire Parnet, Deleuze speaks of the necessity of rendering language strange, and of being a stranger to one's own mother tongue: 'Etre comme un étranger dans sa propre langue. Faire une ligne de fuite.'[1] The line of his argument is slippery (as he admits); the texts he cites, Kafka, Beckett, exist always already between languages, between cultures, yet lead Deleuze to state the desire to become 'bilingue même en une seule langue', to dispossess a language of its singularity, its similarity to itself. We may wonder how these thoughts, and wishes, apply, displaced, to contemporary cinema. Cinema is an art, and an industry, where directors shift more and more easily between languages, nations and locations. In a critical climate which has favoured the charting of national cinemas, where is the place of bilingual film?

This question will be explored in discussion of *La Double Vie de Véronique* (1991), in dialogue with Deleuze.[2] *La Double Vie de Véronique* was Kieślowski's first bilingual film. His position as a Polish director, making a film largely with French money—the film was produced and financed by Sidéral Productions (Paris), Tor Production (Warsaw) and Studio Canal+ (Paris)—and partly in France, was not unambiguous. Compare the thoughts of his compatriot, Andrzej Wajda, in 1981: 'Peut-on rester artiste et créer hors de son pays? Peut-on être écrivain si on est coupé de sa langue? Peut-on être metteur en scène si on est éloigné de son vrai sujet? Je crois que non.'[3] A decade later this is the wager Kieślowski takes up in *La Double Vie de Véronique*. The intervening decade perhaps makes its own difference. Wajda stated, also in 1981: 'ce qui m'intéresse vraiment, c'est de montrer l'origine de certains complexes, des sentiments de la Pologne contemporaine'. This was also the remit, and design, of much of Kieślowski's filmmaking of this period. His early work on documentaries, from his years at the Łódź film school until 1980, demonstrates a desire to make the complexes of his country visible, to record and to testify (despite the weight of censorship). Exemplary in these terms is his *From a Night Porter's Point of View* (1977). In the mid 1970s, Kieślowski turns gradually to making feature films which bear the influence of his documentary work, and it is only in the 1980s that fictional and visual narrative dominate his work.

Rather than seeing a division between the two forms of film-making, Kieślowski posits a continuum. Vincent Amiel quotes him saying: 'Quand je faisais des documentaires, j'étais très près de la vie, des gens vrais. Cela me permettait de savoir comment les gens réagissent, comment ils fonctionnent dans la vie.'[4] This attention to emotion, and to reaction, later informs and nourishes Kieślowski's feature films. If the complexes of Kieślowski's country are made visible in his documentaries, his Polish language films—notably *Camera Buff* (1979), *Blind Chance* (1981) and *No End* (1984), through to the ten short films of *Decalogue* (1988)—themselves work also, arguably, to represent the specificity of Polish concerns within the confines of this decade.[5]

Is there instead a break between Kieślowski's Polish filmmaking and his work, with French funding, in France and Switzerland? *La Double Vie de Véronique*, split between France and Poland, may represent the opening of dialogue between East and West in Europe ironically concretized in the fall of the Berlin Wall and established in Poland gradually at the end of the 1980s, coming together with the bid for a market economy, the legalization of trade unions and the relaxation of censorship. Is the Polish filmmaker, in 1991, in a position ethically (and financially) to remain an artist but to work outside his own country? Does history open the way for the filmmaker to explore difference, and to render his own filmmaking different to itself?

Here it may be important to account for the perspective offered on this question by different critics (from different linguistic back-grounds) who work on Kieślowski. The work of Paul Coates has been particularly important in these terms, since Coates offers discussion of Kieślowski's Polish work in its Polish context, allowing this then to filter his later discussions of Kieślowski's French cinema. This leads to rather different conclusions from those I will develop here. My study will, I hope, show an appropriate awareness of Kieślowski's Polish filmmaking, whilst deliberately focusing on his French cinema and its context. This is not intended to privilege Kieślowski's French cinema over his Polish cinema but rather to draw on the perspective offered by my own critical background in order to precipitate a different reading of this overdetermined, hybrid cinema. In its francophone focus, my work is indebted to the analyses of Kieślowski which have been initiated in the journal *Positif* and pursued in particular by the critic Vincent Amiel. Ironically, however, despite this affiliation with French critical approaches, I am committed to thinking of Kieślowski's cinema as always already double, different and differently indigenous.

The interest of *La Double Vie de Véronique* lies in the fact that both its conditions of production, and its represented subject, frame these issues of bilingual filmmaking directly, yet its final stance, with relation to difference, is unexpected. Indeed the move from Kieślowski's Polish to French cinema is seemingly as seamless as his move from documentary to feature films. *La Double Vie de Véronique* may be read as a pivotal film, allowing the shift from *Decalogue* to the trilogy, incorporating both the Polish and French languages, and produced and designed by both Polish and French workers. *Sight and Sound* published an article with the apt title 'Kieślowski Crossing Over'. Yet the irony of the film is that it depends, precisely, on a narrative of uncanny similarity and resemblance. I will argue, indeed, that *La Double Vie de Véronique* works to recall Kieślowski's Polish filmmaking and simultaneously to look forward to his work in the trilogy in such a way that the difference between the two is denied. Kieślowski works to disrupt the easy mapping of his cinema into separate time bands and national boundaries. His interest is in interference, or, in Deleuze's terms, in the coexistence of separate sheets of past and present in the very body of his filmmaking. In this way temporal and national locations are insistently placed under erasure: Kieślowski's cinema will be seen to present its own re-working of Deleuze's concept of the time-image.

ii The Image

The image itself—its capacities and properties—is the prime abiding concern of Kieślowski's filmmaking. *La Double Vie de Véronique* is a film which takes representation as its subject, and in this it is certainly not singular in Kieślowski's work. Indeed, in the dialogue it creates about representation, *La Double Vie de Véronique* is linked crucially both to what has come before and to what will come after.

Looking backwards to begin with: the film was rendered possible for Kieślowski, and literally afforded, by the international success of *Decalogue* (itself already in part an internationally funded venture). This success led Kieślowski to meet with French producers and to agree to work outside Poland. Beyond this financial and practical link, *Decalogue* and *La Double Vie de Véronique* are also linked both thematically and symbolically. To explain these links necessitates a foray into the exegesis which surrounds *Decalogue*.

There has been much discussion about the relation between the Ten Commandments and the ten short films of *Decalogue*. Christopher Dunkley suggests: 'we are invited to match up a different commandment with each story but [...] I suspect Kieślowski has good reasons for refusing to say which is which.'[6] Dunkley suggests that Kieślowski was not concentrating exclusively on one commandment in the case of each film. Christopher Garbowski, contrarily, while recognizing the interrelation of the separate Commandments, both as they appear in the Old Testament and as they appear in *Decalogue*, demonstrates links between the commandments, as they appear in order, and the chronological series of ten short films. These links depend on the Catholic and Lutheran sequencing.[7] However, anglophone readers of the screenplay of *Decalogue* will be puzzled to find that the text is prefaced by the Ten Commandments in the Anglican sequencing, which necessarily confuses the issue of connection between the separate commandments and films. The Catholic and Lutheran sequencing, seemingly followed in *Decalogue*, does not include a separate interdiction on representation. Paul Coates reminds us importantly of 'the commandment's absorption into the first in the Catholic numbering system'.[8] However, Véronique Campan, depending herself on the Anglican sequencing, comments: 'aucun [film] n'est directement consacré au second commandement: *"Tu ne feras point d'image taillée"*.'[9] She adds: 'Il est paradoxal, pour un montreur d'images, d'*oublier* l'interdit de la représentation.' Her sense of the paradoxical absence of this interdiction in *Decalogue* still holds some resonance, despite her seeming unfamiliarity with the accepted sequencing in Kieślowski's native Poland. But if Kieślowski does not contend directly with this question in *Decalogue* it is perhaps because he makes it his central subject in his subsequent film, *La Double Vie de Véronique*.

The image, and its betrayal of reality, its emptying out of living (or divine) presence, is the central ethical issue of Kieślowski's filmmaking. Following this argument, *La Double Vie de Véronique* may be seen as a missing piece of Kieślowski's Polish filmmaking, of his *Decalogue*, and as a pained meditation on the cult of the image in both Eastern and Western Europe. One of the first images the viewer sees in the film is a vast Soviet statue silhouetted against the sky, driven along in a truck to be destroyed. In a single gesture, Kieślowski illustrates the concrete reality of post-Communist Poland, the falling of its imposed idols and the interdiction on representation which will be the subject of this film.

In his concern with the perils of representation, Kieślowski revisits the territory of his first successful feature film, *Camera Buff*, which demonstrates the ways in which the cinematic medium corrodes and evacuates the subject it chooses, framing it in perpetuity, only to render its actual and temporal disappearance the more painful.

In this film, a factory worker, Filip, buys a small movie camera when his wife has a baby so that he can record the first part of the child's life. His enterprise depends on keeping the past and arresting time. He is slowly led into further filmmaking at the factory where he works, and where he will work on small yet increasingly successful documentary films. Filip becomes obsessed with the ways in which filming and framing allow him ostensibly to control and re-view the world around him. Amiel aptly relates this discovery to Kieślowski himself, noting, as Kieślowski's viewers are sure to, the similarity between the style of Filip's embedded documentary about his fellow worker and the style of Kieślowski's own documentaries.[10] Amiel reads the film as an admission, on Kieślowski's part, of the untenable position of the documentary maker, whose images necessarily transform the reality viewed, making it a spectacle.

What Amiel overlooks is an ambivalence on Kieślowski's part towards imaging and representation of any order. Within the film, Filip eventually loses the very subjects he has set out to represent. His fascination with filming has drawn him, almost imperceptibly, further and further from his wife and child. In the final scene she leaves him, and even here Filip cannot resist watching how her image appears in cinematic terms, framed by the open door. Paul Coates argues: 'At first the wife's estrangement appears unmotivated: not until Filip achieves his limited fame could the camera be said to have come between them. She (like Kieślowski?) appears to subscribe to the ideology that deems the creator an unfeeling monster.'[11] I would disagree in part with Coates's suggestion of a link between the filmmaker's position and that of the wife. The neglect of the wife and child is made apparent in the film by their increasing absence from Filip's frame of vision. Their final departure is surely justified, yet the charge of the film is derived from the only perspective on this departure we are offered, that of Filip whose vision we share. The film's position is double: it refuses to deny the fascination of vision and representation, yet crosscuts this with a recognition of the deleterious personal effects of such artistic practice. Where Kieślowski has expressed his enthusiasm for *La Strada* (1954), like Fellini, he seeks the pathos of revelation after loss and privileges destruction over reparation.

La Double Vie de Véronique returns to the issues in *Camera Buff*, working further, but without resolution, to explore the desire of the artist and necessary betrayal in representation. To look at these questions, and to analyse the status of the image in the film, I will refer to Deleuze's work on cinema, and in particular on the time-image.

iii 'L'Image-cristal'

Vincent Amiel has linked Kieślowski's filmmaking to Deleuze's concept of 'l'image-cristal'. He notes: 'On pourrait dire que le style de Kieślowski est tout entier fondé sur cette "cristallisation" qui met en regard des images d'époques différentes (sans que le recours au flashback soit utile), des images rêvées et des images du réel présent (sans qu'un fondu enchaîné ne serve de "protocole" à ce passage), des images de l'autre et des images de l'un (cf. en particulier *La Double Vie de Véronique*).'[12] He continues, less convincingly, to justify a view of Kieślowski as realist rather than formalist: 'Ce ne sont donc par exemple pas les reflets qui donnent à l'œuvre de Kieślowski sa clé; ce n'est pas seulement le jeu des apparences qui explique leur multiplicité. Ils se comprennent au contraire au sein d'un système plus large qui est celui de la vérité du monde.' It is the question of truth, and of the revelatory power of film, broached here, which is troubling.

In elaborating the concept of the time-image, Deleuze draws on Bergson's theses on time, memory and perception. These Deleuze sums up (conveniently) in the following terms: 'le passé coexiste avec le présent qu'il a été; le passé se conserve en soi, comme passé en général (non-chronologique); le temps se dédouble à chaque instant en présent et passé, présent qui passe et passé qui se conserve.'[13] He reveals how certain films engage with and embody this understanding of time, showing us 'comment nous habitons le temps, comment nous nous mouvons en lui, dans cette forme qui nous emporte, nous ramasse et nous élargit'. But this does not necessarily suggest that these films reveal a truth about time, or *the* truth about the world. Deleuze explores the proximity between a Bergsonian understanding of time and duration and the stylistic and technical developments of modern cinema. For Deleuze, cinema, and his own philosophical approach to cinema, allow the viewer to think through concepts of cinema and concepts addressed by the cinematic medium. Bergson's theses about time afford a new way of thinking about cinema, and cinema itself provides a different medium for exploring the position of the subject in time, and the locating of time in the subject.

Countering Amiel, I contend that Kieślowski's cinema is far from mimetic in any conventional sense. Rather than opening a window onto the world, Kieślowski sets up a mirror to his own filmmaking, reflecting on cinematic representation itself and its capacity to visualize duration, memory and psychic states. This leads him not to reveal a truth of the world, but rather to dissect the ways in which cinematic misrepresentations and distortions can be aligned with mental and psychic misperceptions and delusions. This will be demonstrated with further reference to Deleuze.

Deleuze's study of the time-image is not without its own ambivalences and ambiguities. In his chapter on 'l'image-cristal', he looks at the ways in which film develops the relation between 'une image actuelle' and 'des images-souvenir, des images-rêve, des images-monde'. He shows how modern cinema has moved beyond the use of specific devices: flashbacks, fades, slow motion and so on, which clearly signal the distinction between the actual and the virtual. Modern cinema renders these divisions and distinctions increasingly unclear, and stresses the entire equivalence of actual and virtual. The 'image-cristal' may still represent or reflect two orders of representation, two incommensurable sets of images, but it renders the relation between them, and their hierarchy, uncertain and unstable. Deleuze explains: '[l'indiscernabilité] ne supprime pas la distinction des deux faces, mais la rend inassignable, chaque face prenant le rôle de l'autre dans une relation qu'il faut qualifier de présupposition réciproque, ou de réversibilité'. Ironically, in its objective status 'l'image-cristal' works to undo our perceptions about the objective apprehension of reality: 'l'indiscernabilité du réel et de l'imaginaire, ou du présent et du passé, de l'actuel et du virtuel, ne se produit donc nullement dans la tête ou dans l'esprit, mais est le caractère objectif de certaines images existantes, doubles par nature'.

Deleuze makes reference to the mirror, to its use in films, and to its capacity to undo the veracity and verisimilitude of the image. He writes: 'l'image en miroir est virtuelle par rapport au personnage actuel que le miroir saisit, mais elle est actuelle dans le miroir qui ne laisse plus au personnage qu'une simple virtualité et le repousse hors champ.' Deleuze suggests that the use of an optical device, the mirror, and its circuit of reflections, works to distort and change the possibilities of reading a film and construing its meaning. He argues: 'Quand les images virtuelles prolifèrent ainsi, leur ensemble absorbe toute l'actualité du personnage, en même temps que le personnage n'est plus qu'une virtualité parmi les autres.' Deleuze provides a seeming blueprint for understanding the relation between mirroring, identity and the virtual status of protagonists in cinema. It is in terms of this exploration of the image and virtuality that his work will be useful here. Nevertheless, some caution is needed in considering the adoption of his theory to elucidate the properties of the image in recent film.

For Deleuze, the proliferation of virtual images of which he speaks is found 'à l'état pur dans le célèbre palais des glaces de *La Dame de Shanghai*'. A problem arises in part from Deleuze's use of specific (historical) examples. We may ask whether the time-image itself can ever be more than temporally and historically contingent, its meaning dependent (in Deleuze's formulation) on its place in film history and its time of viewing. In this sense, when a filmmaker such as Woody Allen alludes to *The Lady from Shanghai* (1948) in *Manhattan Murder Mystery* (1993) and re-creates its play of mirrors (or the play of mistaken identity of *Vertigo* (1958)) the viewer may feel primarily that *Manhattan Murder Mystery* reveals the over-determination of cinematic images, and their paradoxical loss of primary meaning. Perhaps the time-image of modern cinema is temporally specific, even stylistically recognizable? Is it now being eroded by an 'image-hommage' of postmodernity? What is the fate of the 'image-cristal' in Kieślowski's intensely overdetermined cinema?

Where Deleuze uses the term 'l'image-cristal', his references to crystal itself (despite allusions to Zanussi's *The Structure of Crystals* (1969)) remain largely figurative. The image of crystal offers Deleuze a device by which the structural overlayering of reflections and the transposition of actual and virtual images in modern cinema can be theorized and effectively fixed. What is evident is that Kieślowski is interested in a more literal interpretation of the 'image-cristal'. The reflections in mirrors on which Deleuze comments in Welles and Losey have been all but replaced, in Kieślowski, by reflections in glass, by phantom reflections which haunt his films' actual images, with ghostly effect. This is one of the distinctive stylistic features of Kieślowski's filmmaking; its effects are felt throughout the body of his films, although this feature is exaggerated as his career progresses. Is this stylistic device evidence of an overinvestment in the aesthetic properties of the image as Kieślowski's filmmaking becomes further divorced from the context in which it was first produced? Or does Kieślowski's literal representation of the 'image-cristal', his different take on Deleuze's theory in effect, allow us to think about the direction cinema might be taking post the time-image?

Deleuze overlooks questions relating to psychoanalytic theory in his work on cinema. He passes quickly over the question of 'l'indiscernabilité du réel et de l'imaginaire'. Surely it is of interest that this condition (whereby the individual, a viewer, is unable effectively to perceive the difference between the real and the imaginary) has been pathologized and is deemed the symptom of a psychic disorder. In his essay 'The "Uncanny"', Freud argues that 'an uncanny effect is often and easily produced when the distinction between imagination and reality is effaced'.[14] He continues: 'The infantile element in this, which also dominates the minds of neurotics, is the over-accentuation of psychical reality in comparison with material reality.' By implication the viewer of the 'image-cristal' is put in the position of the neurotic who is unable to perceive the distinction between psychical and material reality.

This raises the issue whether, in those films which self-consciously and visually refuse the difference between the real and the imaginary, a distinction might be made between those which give some semblance of restoring order, and sorting virtual and actual (such as *Vertigo*), and those which do not. There may be greater interest in those films which allow no resolution of the conflict of virtual and actual, multiplying associations and allowing no resolution, as is the case of Resnais's *L'Année dernière à Marienbad* (1961) as cited by Deleuze, or indeed as is the case of *La Double Vie de Véronique*.

The former class of films (and of course any rigid distinction or definition remains difficult) are no less examples of 'l'image-cristal' than the latter, but their relation to psychoanalytic discourse is different, as is their effect on the spectator. The latter set of films, those which offer no final distinction between real and imaginary, construct effectively their own specific cinema of psychosis. In this sense these films might be said to foster not only an unstable view of the relations between film and reality, but an unstable view of reality itself.

This raises a further question of whose view of reality we are discussing. In *Cinéma 2: L'Image-temps* there is almost no discussion of the vicissitudes of spectatorship, an issue which, for the past two decades, has been practically central in Anglo-American film theory.[15] Indeed, as D. N. Rodowick remarks with fine irony: 'although he is the most sophisticated twentieth century philosopher of difference, Deleuze seems to have little to offer on the problem of difference in spectatorship. Despite some powerful pages on cinemas of decolonization, he has little to say specifically on questions of sexual, racial and class difference.'[16] We may wonder about the role and experience of the spectator with relation to the 'image-cristal'. Where an ideal, or virtual, spectator may actualize in her viewing experience the series of mergers and moves between real and imaginary, past and present, dream and fantasy, that the film may reflect in its structure and surface images, there can be no guarantee that any specific spectator will accept the series of distortions of perception a film offers. This raises the question of a risk of the spectator's attempt to find logic and veracity where the filmmaker has left lacunae and doubt; this risk must necessarily increase in proportion to the very indecipherability of a particular film. And I would argue that this has specifically been the fate of *La Double Vie de Véronique* where viewers attempt to understand a film which simply does not make sense.

But this question apart, does Deleuze account sufficiently for the impact on the viewer of a cinema of psychosis? His work never focuses on the loss and disorientation of the viewer whose stability of perception is disrupted. In writing about mirrors and the disruption of actual and virtual in cinema, Deleuze neglects the possibility that the screen itself functions as mirror, reflecting back a distorted reflection with which the viewer may come to identify.[17] Where much important work in spectatorship theory has concentrated on classic narrative cinema, and latterly on genre films and specifically horror, further work needs to be done on the psychic complexities of viewing those recent films which create a paranoid position for the viewer, in self-consciously reflecting her position within the narrative and visual apparatus of the film. But here my concern is only, explicitly, with Kieślowski's (paranoid) spectator and how she finds herself in the images in crystal in his films.

I want to return to *La Double Vie de Véronique*, but to keep in mind the issues in dialogue with Deleuze I have outlined here, namely: the possibility that the time-image will itself become a recognizable cinematic device, recalled rather than created in films, to become in effect an 'image-hommage'; the possibility, meaning and difference of a literal 'image-cristal' or image in crystal; the primacy of those films which refuse the ultimate definition of the virtual and the actual, and, related to this, the risks of such a cinema of psychosis; and finally the effect on the viewer of the 'image-cristal' and vice versa. How far does *La Double Vie de Véronique* provide a medium which focuses these specific questions?

iv Titles Sequence

Intercut with the titles sequence of *La Double Vie de Véronique* are several shots which are not seen again through the course of the film. The viewer is invited, at this liminal moment, to look at images through glass. The images are shot (as) from a moving vehicle, or through layers of consciousness: they have a distorted, almost sepia quality. We make out a young woman walking along; it is perhaps her moving shape that we notice most. She is seen then in a square bending down, pigeons and commotion around her. At this juncture the viewer has no stable point of reference for the images (whether she will ever have one is another matter). Before the titles sequence, we have seen and heard two separate brief episodes where a mother talks to a child, one in Polish and one in French. The very opening shots of the film are seen inverted as a child hangs upside down.[18] In the second scene a small child, remarkably similar to the first one we see, but not identical, looks through a magnifying glass at the veins on a leaf. The only link between these two sequences and the images shot from a moving vehicle is the possible interest in distorted imagery.

It is only later in the film that the images from the titles sequence begin to be inserted into some narrative or visual trajectory. I think it would be realistic to say that on a first viewing the images from the titles sequence have been completely forgotten by the time they appear to be inserted into the narrative. How unconscious recollection may work to create a sensation of uncanny familiarity for the viewer as she encounters the images again is another matter. The desire to create this effect may motivate the more overt use of flash-forwards in films such as *Decalogue 1* and *Trois Couleurs: Blanc*.

In looking at the supposed flashforward in the titles sequence of *La Double Vie de Véronique*, what is telling is the slight discrepancy the viewer may begin to perceive between the liminal images and their point of reference in the film. Inserting these images, shot behind glass, in his titles sequence, Kieślowski works overtly to draw our attention to the single most important scene in the film. This is the scene which records the only direct interference (that we witness) between the lives of Weronika and Véronique, the film's two protagonists. Their paths cross once, in a square in Kraków. Up until this point in the narrative we have followed the history and largely shared the point of view of Weronika, a Polish singer who lives with her father and goes to visit her aunt who is mysteriously ill in Kraków. During this visit, Weronika, clutching manuscript pages of music, walks through the square in Kraków in the middle of a demonstration. Her music is knocked out of her hands, and for this reason she bends down, but this does not prevent her then seeing a young French woman, who is part of a foreign tour, being herded back onto a bus and taking photos from the window.

What Weronika and the viewer come to recognize is that this young French woman is Weronika's double. They are played in the film by the same actress, Irène Jacob, and appear all but identical.[19] The point of meeting is most significant, perhaps, because it is only experienced consciously here by Weronika who, whilst noticing her double, goes unnoticed by her. Despite Weronika's hesitant smile of recognition as she sees her own image, Véronique acts in the film as Weronika's Doppelgänger who stands as a harbinger of death. Weronika dies soon, at the twenty-seventh minute of the film,[20] of heart failure as she sings a verse from Dante.

The fact that Véronique contrarily never appears to see her double becomes uncanny when we realize that the opening image in the titles sequence, the view of the young woman we now come to recognize as Weronika in the square, is shot supposedly from Véronique's point of view. The viewer is faced with one of the film's puzzles. We never see Véronique catching sight of Weronika: we can only assume that she is still on the tourbus as Weronika drops the music, and thus in a position at least potentially to view the scene. As she is witnessed and recognized later by Weronika she is standing in the square with her compatriots taking photos. Latterly she seems to move blindly onto the bus, continuing to take an almost random series of pictures. We are later given evidence which suggests that the scene of 'meeting herself' has gone entirely unremarked by Véronique. Far later in the film, when she has been courted and seduced by the marionettist Alexandre Fabbri, he looks at the black and white prints of photographs she has taken on a tour in Eastern Europe and he recognizes the image of Weronika, believing it, it seems, to be Véronique. We are led to suppose, by Véronique's surprise and emotion, that she has never seen or looked closely at this alien image of herself. It is only now with Alexandre that she sees her own double. This appears to prove that the view from the bus window is not, consciously at least, that of Véronique.

But what is the status of the images in the titles sequence? Do they represent what Véronique has seen but not consciously recognized (in much the same way that images in many films, and in this film too, pass unremarked by their viewers)? Or does Kieślowski present us at this juncture with another point of view, with the point of view of the camera which shadows but does not consciously coincide with that of the protagonist? What is the implication of this image shot behind glass? As we view the film more and more consciously I think it becomes clearer that Kieślowski is intent on creating a discourse about the image, and most specifically about the image viewed through glass, the image reflected in glass, in translucent material and in reflective surfaces. *La Double Vie de Véronique* might be used to construct an inventory of such virtual images which exist, quite literally for the viewer, as 'images-cristal'.

In some senses Kieślowski is true to Deleuze's definition of the 'image-cristal': in his correlation of images shot through glass and images reflected in glass, he would seem to associate the virtual and the actual, and to remind us that the cinematic image itself, where a view is focused through a lens, necessarily involves an act of mediated vision and consequent derealization. But where Kieślowski surpasses Deleuze, in the first place, is in his fascination with the very reflexive material, the substances in his films—glass, water, plastic, crystal—through which images are seen and in which images are reflected. In this respect, Kieślowski's filmmaking is at its most stylized and he comes to achieve, in perhaps equal proportions, the alienation and seduction of his viewers.

There is tremendous pleasure to be found in the optical illusions of *La Double Vie de Véronique*, and possible significance in the play of reflections. It is through this play that Kieślowski establishes a discourse about self-reflexivity and representation. Take for example the

scene where Weronika travels on a train to Kraków and looks out of
the train window: we see what appears to be a clearly focused scene
whose centre gradually dissolves and distorts.[21] It becomes clear to the
viewer that the glass of the train window is warped and is literally
distorting our vision. To add to this effect, Weronika takes a small glass
or crystal ball from her bag and holds it up to the window so that we
see the view now reflected and inverted through the convex substance
of the ball. The spatial relations of the image are distorted here too
(and the viewer is reminded perhaps of the inverted images the child
Weronika sees). Reflected and distorted thus, the image on the screen
takes on the properties of a mirrored reflection in a Flemish painting.
This effect is enhanced since the view itself represents a small town
and a red church with a fine spire and buildings around: an image itself
seemingly familiar from the paintings of Van Eyck. The image is also
one which appears as an etching on the wall in Weronika's house, we
assume drawn by her father since we see him working intently on
another such picture, a magnifying lens fitted over his eye. We may
surmise that this is the scene of which Véronique later dreams, un-
aware of its provenance. (An irony here is that where the film's viewer
is tempted to interpret this as further evidence of the uncanny link
between Weronika and Véronique, where one receives the other's
mental images, in fact there is every possibility, within the logic of the
narrative, that Véronique saw this very image on her trip through
Poland and that it surfaces from her own rather than her double's
unconscious). Where the scene itself may be of little significance, it is
its proliferation and re-presentation in the film which gain interest for
the viewer.

Kieślowski's aesthetic position here appears not far removed from
that of the grandmother of Proust's narrator in *A la recherche du temps
perdu*. As the narrator reveals: 'Elle eût aimé que j'eusse dans ma
chambre des photographies des monuments ou des paysages les plus
beaux. Mais au moment d'en faire l'emplette, et bien que la chose
représentée eût une valeur esthétique, elle trouvait que la vulgarité,
l'utilité reprenaient trop vite leur place dans le mode mécanique de
représentation, la photographie. Elle essayait de ruser et, sinon
d'éliminer entièrement la banalité commerciale, du moins de la
réduire, d'y substituer, pour la plus grande partie, de l'art encore, d'y
introduire plusieurs "épaisseurs" d'art.'[22] It might be argued that *La
Double Vie de Véronique* ironically demonstrates its own distrust and
even contempt for the mechanically produced work of art, and works

in effect to inflect the photographic image in such a way that its artistic qualities are self-consciously privileged.[23]

This leads to the question whether Kieślowski can be said to offer his own distorted view of the 'image-cristal'. In *La Double Vie de Véronique* the indiscernibility of the virtual and the actual appears to provoke a loss of meaning, and a loss of a stable relation to reality, losses which are themselves significant. This can be explored most effectively in relation to the thematics of doubling and uncanny resemblance which the film takes in its title and places at its centre. A noticeable visual pleasure of the film is indeed that the double life of Véronique appears to be illustrated literally and playfully throughout the film. When Weronika tells her father, mysteriously, that she has the sense that she is not alone, the viewer is in a position entirely to concur with this view.

In the first part of the film in particular, almost every time we see Weronika she is not alone, but shadowed by her reflection in photographs, in glass doors, in windows. Even as her boyfriend makes love to her in the first honey-lit interior of the film, the camera focuses on Weronika's tranquil face and the object of her gaze, the photograph of herself which looks almost tenderly over the scene as ripples of light from the falling rain play over its surface. In the pleasure of her body, Weronika seems yet within the thrall of a mirroring relation to herself, to herself as image and other. We see always already a double image of Weronika, before it becomes evident, as the narrative unfolds, that she has her own living double. In this sense, the double life of Weronika is, in the first place, a visual illusion, a shadowing of the supposedly actual by the virtual, and an insistent reminder that we as viewers are sharing the camera's view of a constructed and artificial image.

v Parallels

This interpretation sits uneasily with those readings of the film which are more spiritual in nature. Critics account differently for the mystery at the centre of the film.[24] In the same issue of *Sight and Sound* there are two differing interpretations. Tony Rayns suggests that the film starts from a '"fantastic" premise: that if many people in the world are fundamentally very similar, why shouldn't there be two who are, in fact, identical?'.[25] Jonathan Romney is more speculative, writing: 'The story may be about one woman with a double life, about two women with one life between them, or about two entirely separate lives.'[26] Kieślowski himself is hardly more explanatory when he says in interview in *Positif*: 'Un film sur deux vies: la vie là-bas et la vie ici bien qu'elles soient pareilles'.[27] This description brings us closer to the analysis I want to hazard here. Alain Masson suggests, also in *Positif*, 'L'histoire de Weronika n'est que l'anticipation de l'histoire de Véronique'.[28] Masson sees the film depending on the type of parallels found already in Kieślowski's earlier *Blind Chance* and it is this reading which I find the most persuasive, for reasons I shall outline below.

This very issue of parallelism is crucial to the film. The parallel existences the film takes as its subject work on a formal level as exercises in narration, as two different ways of telling the same story. In this reading of *La Double Vie de Véronique* Kieślowski may be seen to offer two alternative accounts of the same history, in different locations, with the slightest 'décalage horaire' but with easily recognizable similarities. Yet this is still not quite what we find in *La Double Vie de Véronique*. *Blind Chance*, cited by Masson (above), offers, quite literally, three different tellings of the same story where the narrative works in triplicate, focusing on three different paths an individual's life might take as the outcome of a single, seemingly random event. In each of the re-tellings, entire equivalence is supposed and we are given a sense of observing the virtual realities of an individual's life. *Blind Chance* is a moving exploration of chance, choice and destiny. Kieślowski uses the film form to dramatize and view the footsteps which echo in both memory and imagination; the film's narrative strands become so many passages which might be taken. *La Double Vie de Véronique* is neither so clear-cut nor so philosophically engaged. It chooses instead, I would argue, to make hypotheses an integral part of the viewer's experience and to engage the viewer in a series of questions about its possible meanings. Thus the film draws attention to the way it exists as virtual object which will be actualized in very different ways by its various viewers. This bid for multiplicity appears witnessed itself in Kieślowski's unrealized desire to make seventeen almost imperceptibly different cuts of the film and show a different one in each of the seventeen cinemas where the film premiered in Paris.

John Kim, a critic sensitive to the multivalency and open-endedness of Kieślowski's films, suggests that for Kieślowski the ultimate truth is sometimes not needed. He argues: 'Some may question Kieślowski's open-ended closings, suggesting that he misses making a deeper point with his films by leaving the situation without any sort of final conclusion. Yet this is exactly where Kieślowski reaches his greatest, and most poetic, height.'[29] Yet even for Kim, Kieślowski is, in this inconclusiveness, 'a visionary whose cinema has lightened some of the darker corners of existence'. Where visual pleasure is concerned, and the very sensuality of the light in Kieślowski's images, I agree with Kim, yet I would modify his statement to say that Kieślowski has lit up, rather than lightened, some of the darker corners of existence.

No critic has read *La Double Vie de Véronique* as a film about betrayal, yet this, in my view, is its parting emotion. Despite the sumptuous golden lighting of the film, its amniotic tranquillity and the very pleasure of watching Irène Jacob's face and body viewed and reflected, it remains, for me, a film of loss, regression and erosion. This interpretation, which I will explore further below, will be related specifically, again, to the thematics of representation and Kieślowski's manipulation of the 'image-cristal'.

VI Homages

The ways in which *La Double Vie de Véronique* recalls and records images from other films merits further discussion. I am not so much interested here in looking at the multiple ways in which Kieślowski borrows from or pays homage to his fellow filmmakers, as concerned to demonstrate how the image, in *La Double Vie de Véronique,* is always already cinematic. The doubling to which Kieślowski refers in the film's title is essentially the doubling of reality in film.

One of the first images we see of Weronika is itself strangely familiar. She lifts her head upwards, her eyes closed, her hands clasping her face. The image recalls one of the most arresting images of Andie McDowell from Stephen Soderbergh's *Sex, lies and videotape* (1989). The reference is no coincidence since Kieślowski has referred to his initial desire to cast McDowell as Véronique, and to his fascination with her gestures and with her particular manner of holding her hands to her face. Véronique's gesture finds its double in another film. That it should be a film which itself takes filming as subject, and the imbrication of video art in an individual's erotic life, seems only apt. We gain some impression of the overlayering of connotative meanings in the film, its games with the viewer. But this is a film which is read as one of resurrection, and offers a definitive scene in the aptly named Gare St Lazare. This is a film where the heroine's very name, Veronica, refers us to a hagiographic instance of representation, and to the possibility of flouting the interdiction on imaging in the very tactile impression of the flesh. The film leaves the viewer in this sense disoriented by or perhaps even indifferent to its ever reflecting, yet overdetermined meanings. Amiel justly refers to the systems of Peter Greenaway's filmmaking when he works to find a comparative point of reference for Kieślowski. But does this render *La Double Vie de Véronique* a mere *jeu d'apparences* and intellectual game? I think not, because the film acknowledges the dangers of the game it is playing. This leads us to the ways in which Kieślowski may be seen to insert *La Double Vie de Véronique* into the tradition of French cinema, and particularly that which emerged in and around the *Nouvelle Vague*, in the work of Rohmer, Resnais and Godard (directors all discussed by Deleuze in *Cinéma 2: L'Image-temps*).

As a setting for the main part of the French section of *La Double Vie de Véronique* Kieślowski chooses Clermont-Ferrand. He justifies this choice by saying: 'Nous avons choisi Clermont-Ferrand (dont il reste assez peu dans le film) parce que la ville est bâtie sur un rocher volcanique assez gris, comme Cracovie.'[30] The reason seems clear enough and it is certain that Kieślowski and his production team have achieved a remarkable visual resemblance between the separate national and geographic locations of the film (the use of colour filters playing some part in this). But in choosing Clermont-Ferrand Kieślowski chooses the location of Rohmer's film *Ma Nuit chez Maud* (1969) and in this choice, surely, there is no coincidence.[31] Rohmer's film is literally recalled, visually, at a certain point in *La Double Vie de Véronique*: Véronique, now in love with the marionettist, has gone to look in a bookshop window and sees the titles through the glass. The *mise-en-scène* is very similar to a scene in *Ma Nuit chez Maud* where the narrator, played by Jean-Louis Trintignant (who will reappear in Kieślowski's French cinema), looks through a bookshop window. Resemblance is enhanced by the view in both films of Clermont-Ferrand in December, with almost identical starry Christmas decorations illuminated against a night sky. Why does Kieślowski create these visual echoes? If he is attempting to define himself with relation to French filmmaking, as I believe he is, why does he choose this particular film?

My discussion here has centred so far on the Polish section of *La Double Vie de Véronique*; in turning to address its French mirror image, it is tempting to look at the differences and divergences between the two sections. The French section is, largely, a love story and a tale of marionettes (the latter not featuring at all in the Polish prelude). The theme of the marionette theatre, and its moving puppets, is apt if we consider that Kieślowski is exploring the uncanny in Freudian terms. The automaton (and marionette), giving the appearance of life, aping and doubling a moving figure, is, of course, one of the physical instances of the uncanny to which Freud refers.[32] If the marionette itself is perceived to disturb the boundaries between real and imaginary, psychical and material reality, its place in *La Double Vie de Véronique* is again overdetermined. And the very dramas which Alexandre Fabbri, the marionettist, enacts with his puppets are themselves apt.

Véronique first falls under his spell as she watches his show in the school hall with her small pupils. He performs a tale of death and metamorphosis: a ballet dancer, an ethereal performer, dies (like Weronika) mid-performance. But, by a sleight of hand, she is transformed, to rise out of her shroud resurrected as a butterfly. This first tale appears to have an uncanny resonance within Véronique's own unknown story (although whether it is a barely perceptible intimation of this which draws her to Alexandre is left unexplained). Her reasons for eventually rejecting him and returning to her father are, it seems, far clearer. Near the end of the film a series of point-of-view shots and a moving camera lead Véronique ominously and relentlessly down the corridor of Alexandre's apartment into his workshop where she finds him creating a new series of puppets which uncannily resemble Véronique herself. This episode comes after Alexandre's discovery of Véronique's double in the Polish photo. When she questions him as to why there are double puppets he gives at first a feeble excuse: he handles the puppets a lot as he performs and they are quickly damaged. But then he relents and begins to explain to Véronique the tale he will tell with the puppets. Two girls are identical and do not know each other, yet their lives intersect uncannily so that the second will learn by the mistakes of the first. He tells Véronique that this puppet show will be called *La Double Vie de* .... It is this appropriation of her life that Véronique flees, betrayed, at the end of the film.

Alexandre's virtual puppet show relates closely to Kieślowski's actual film. If the second puppet show functions as an internal reflection within the film it appears to reveal, as in *Camera Buff*, how fiction or re-enactment entraps, yet displaces the reality it doubles.

La Double Vie de Véronique appears here to take as its subject the very reification of representation which is revealed in particularly graphic terms as Véronique is rendered an inanimate puppet in Alexandre's marionette show. Perhaps this is also the fate of Irène Jacob in Kieślowski's film?

A similar play between reality and representation is explored with the same actress in *Trois Couleurs: Rouge* where Jacob, here playing the model Valentine, is photographed for an advertising hoarding which is hung over Geneva. At the very end of the film, as the Judge watches television and discovers that, miraculously, Valentine is a survivor of the ferry accident to which he has unwittingly led her, he sees her image in profile and, although she is moving, she is seen suddenly in the same position and image as the advertisement itself (leaving the viewer again with an experience of uncanny similarity). The Judge in *Rouge* is himself an image of the film director who attempts to manipulate and pull the strings of the characters around him. His failure and fear seem to be the subject of *Rouge* as Kieślowski dwells on the perils of representation. The image of the filmmaker as puppeteer already has its own resonance in *La Double Vie de Véronique*. The viewer is faced with the possibility, even likelihood, that Kieślowski reflects upon his own practice in the art of Alexandre Fabbri. And it is in this way that Kieślowski's links with Rohmer may be clarified.

Deleuze has commented on the ways in which 'l'image automatique exige une nouvelle conception du rôle ou de l'acteur, mais aussi de la pensée elle-même'.[33] He suggests that Dreyer creates '[une] momie [...] coupée d'un monde extérieur trop rigide, trop pesant ou trop superficiel', and he adds: 'elle n'en était pas moins pénétrée de sentiments'. He continues, however: 'chez Rohmer, la momie fait place à une marionette, en même temps que les sentiments font place à une "idée", obsédante, qui va l'inspirer du dehors, quitte à l'abandonner pour la rendre au vide'. Where Deleuze speaks of how the actor and character are conceived in Rohmer's cinema, note too that a drama of manipulation is frequently found reflected at the centre of the plots of Rohmer's films. Where the filmmaker seems to conceive of his characters as marionettes, his films demonstrate that the characters who themselves share this delusion fall victim to their misconception and their misapprehension of the autonomy of the other. And this is entirely the case in *Ma Nuit chez Maud*.

Rohmer's film is not, in general terms, closely linked to *La Double*

Vie de Véronique. What it does afford, however, is a discourse about misreading and misapprehension which proves salutary in a reading of Kieślowski's film. Considering *Ma Nuit chez Maud* we see that the narrator has been so intent on the construction of his life as marionette theatre that he has misconceived the role that his future wife Françoise plays and has been blind to her implication in the night of adultery he conceives but never finally achieves with Maud. His experience on the beach at the end of the film is entirely unsettling as he learns that Françoise knew Maud all along, precisely because Françoise played the other woman in the drama of infidelity which separated Maud from her husband. He learns, in a sense, that Françoise was always already there even before he approached her in the town in Clermont-Ferrand, and that she was where he did not expect to find her. In more conventional terms, he finds that her blond Catholic purity, and his ideal of faithful love, have been an illusion, that she is not what she seems. As so often in Rohmer's films, the viewer is made party, through intense dialogue, to one character's view of events, only to become aware in the course of the film's diegesis that in fact appearances are deceptive and these mental images are entirely deluded. A redemptive (and faithful) view of Rohmer would suggest that truth is established in the film's dénouement together with a revelation of error; another view would tend towards the belief that one series of misconceptions gives way to another, and, further, that the filmmaker cannot entirely escape the fostering of illusion of the very medium in which he works.

But what about Kieślowski in this? If Rohmer displays the unsuccessful manipulation of others, and makes the viewer party to the play of deception on which his films depend, what relation to Rohmer's cinema does Kieślowski establish by quoting from *Ma Nuit chez Maud*? I would argue that in this way Kieślowski draws into question the very ontology of the cinematic image. Where Rohmer, following Bazin up to a certain point, appears both to establish and to place under erasure the stable relation between the filmic image and the reality it represents, Kieślowski, quoting Rohmer, puts realism in cinema entirely under attack, and constructs a nexus of relations in his film which work to suggest that the cinematic image draws always and ever on other representations, becoming, in effect, the 'image-hommage' I have mentioned above.

Yet Kieślowski is far from the postmodern artifice of the *cinéma du look*, for example. His cinema is profoundly a cinema of regret and it is in this sense that discussion of *La Double Vie de Véronique* may allow us to enter again into dialogue with Deleuze's work on the time-image. In creating an implicit 'image-hommage' in *La Double Vie de Véronique* Kieślowski allows different sheets of cinematic past to coexist in his films. Coming from outside, Kieślowski's cinema avoids the intense generational influence which can be witnessed in individual national cinemas, but allows instead, in a Deleuzian sense, a temporal perspective which emphasizes coexistence and simultaneity rather than relentless forward movement. Yet rather than acclaiming the layers of allusion it constructs, Kieślowski's work appears paradoxically to emphasize the very loss of meaning in citation.

La Double Vie de Véronique explores an over-layering of virtual images and creates a continuum between reflected images and cinematic images: it is in these terms that we might define the self-reflexivity of Kieślowski's cinema. Cinematic images, scenes copied from other films, become so many 'images-souvenir' which allow different levels of cinematic, visual and virtual reality to co-exist. Yet what the film appears to embody ultimately is not technical or philosophical virtuosity, but emotional disturbance. In the double history of Véronique which Kieślowski projects cinematically, he takes more account than Deleuze himself of the disorientation and potential loss which accompany both the separation and the indiscernibility of the virtual and the actual.

Deleuze, following Bergson, considers that time is double and doubled in every instant, yet he does not dwell specifically on the division between the 'présent qui passe' and the 'passé qui se conserve'. The necessary *décalage* and its attendant sense of loss (and disorientation) goes unremarked. For Kieślowski, the possible difference between the actual present which is lost and the virtual image of time which is preserved appears of extreme importance. He allows this doubling of time to be re-thought in the doubling of an existence. Véronique, following Weronika in the film's diegesis, appears as the virtual image of the actual woman we have viewed and known in the first part of the film. And Véronique repeatedly suffers her own virtual status. Her experiences with Alexandre are prime evidence of this.

When, following Alexandre's series of clues, virtual recordings and props, Véronique arrives in the place where he has waited for her, and effectively performed her choreographed role, she believes, it seems, that he has drawn her to him through love. When she asks why he has manipulated her thus, he replies that he wanted to see if it was possible, psychologically, for a woman to make the series of moves Véronique has made. He is, in a sense, testing the plot of a novel. For Véronique, each actual move has been rendered virtual as she finds herself ensnared in a fiction of Alexandre's making: her responses have been inspired by an illusion. She is the victim of his seduction. She will be pursued by Alexandre, and apparently desired by him, precisely because she feels pain at his deception: we may assume that her actual pain will be rendered virtual and preserved in his representation. The viewer may be seduced by Alexandre's seduction of Véronique, yet a lingering doubt should remain, I think, as their love unfolds. Can we be certain that in his every move, even after his revelation to Véronique, Alexandre does not continue to choreograph her actions and test her responses?

For Véronique, and for the viewer, the intentions and desires of the marionettist remain to the last indeterminate. He is shown to play literally with the indiscernibility of the actual and virtual in his courting of Véronique. His love is an experiment, as is Kieślowski's film. Describing Rohmer, as we have seen, Deleuze suggests that Rohmer's characters become puppets and simultaneously that emotion and feelings in his films give way to 'une "idée", obsédante'. Kieślowski's filmmaking ostensibly, and self-consciously, follows in this tradition, governed by its own discourse on representation, on doubling and imaging. The irony of the film lies in the fact that Kieślowski is not content to replicate the dominance of thought over feeling, or idea over emotion, in the construction and diegesis of his films. Rather he makes that loss of emotion his very subject.

VII Interference

La Double Vie de Véronique works as an experiment in different layers of narrative, and levels of representation. Kieślowski demonstrates how a Polish film might be made of the life of Weronika, and a French film of the life of Véronique. The two strands of the film exist as part of a formal exercise or experiment. The importance of this aspect of the film, and its implied discourse about the relative similarity of East and West in Europe between 1966 (date of birth of both women) and the present should not be underestimated. If the film followed the pattern and example of *Blind Chance* this similarity might be seen as its ultimate message. Yet, as we are reminded from the titles sequence onwards, Kieślowski is interested here, over and above parallelism, in interference.

The issue of interference surfaces again in *Rouge* where Kieślowski allows an uncertain relation to exist between the Judge and his seeming alter ego, Auguste. It seems that Auguste is living out the Judge's destiny, that the Judge is in a position to witness and in part choreograph the existence of a character who embodies his own past. Logical explanations of the uncanny resemblances between the Judge's memory of the past (which still exists in the present) and Auguste's present (which is becoming past as he exists) remain impossible. Likewise, logical explanations remain impossible in *La Double Vie de Véronique*. But this is because Kieślowski's is a cinema of hypothesis which attempts to project our 'images-rêve' and 'images-souvenir' whilst reminding us, ironically, of their specific ephemerality.

The virtual supersedes the actual in Kieślowski's cinema. This can be related to his predilection for virtual images, the dominance of cinematic citations and his refusal of (actual) logic. While continually showing us the virtual images of actual reality which film as medium records, Kieślowski draws on the interplay of virtual and actual on which cinema depends. Yet in comparison with Rohmer, I have argued that Kieślowski explores a collapse of realism (and the denial of the actual this collapse necessitates). This collapse is not immediately apparent to Kieślowski's viewers, it seems, and herein lies a further betrayal which is the product of his cinematic practice.

Kieślowski's cinema is one which plays with the viewer's notions of legibility. He makes use of the ostensible, concrete and now clichéd signs of Hitchcock's cinema (as redeployed also by Rohmer). Weronika, for example, dreams that she is running down a street which is in fact marked by a no entry sign. The images which represent this dream to the viewer are entirely continuous in quality and style with the other images of this part of the film. It is only as we hear Weronika's narration to her father of the events as part of a dream narrative that we realize that actual and virtual have here been rendered indiscernible. This might be an instance where we note the resemblance between Kieślowski's cinema and Deleuze's concept of the time-image. Yet the self-consciousness of the image, signalled in its overt use of the cinematic device, the road sign, leads us to an awareness of the artifice of the technique. Surely Kieślowski's cinema draws our attention to the re-thinking of time, image and legibility in modern cinema. In this sense, viewing itself becomes effectively a process of recognition, but this again is entirely reflected in the very thematics of this filmic narrative.

Kieślowski's viewer is made aware of the devices by which the virtual and actual are inter-related. His cinema is innovative, however, in its attempt to think beyond this specific binary (in Deleuzian terms) and to explore the doubling relation between virtual images. In this sense Kieślowski's cinema is specifically vertiginous, and tests the possibility of perpetually disrupting the viewer's response. Where we have seen the proliferation of representations of the town viewed through crystal, there are further uncertain images with which Véronique's viewer is faced, and here it will be seen that it is not so much doubleness as doubling that is Kieślowski's obsession.

Weronika, as character, exists as virtual image of the actual actress Irène Jacob (whose voice is dubbed into Polish). The virtual image of Irène Jacob is itself perpetually doubled visually as we see the series of reflections which ghost the image of Weronika. But in the square in Kraków we discover that Weronika has her own living double, embodied in the figure of Véronique, a further virtual image of Irène Jacob.[34] Weronika and Véronique exist in the film effectively and visually as reflections of one another. And this virtual status is explored further by Alexandre in the second part of the film where he first makes Véronique a virtual reflection of a character in his projected fiction (a virtual reality), and then proceeds to appropriate a virtual story of her existence for the purposes of his puppet theatre. This perpetuating *mise-en-abyme* is itself enhanced by the further series of reflections between the filmmaker's own practice, the very title of his film, and the projected puppet show which is at once the film's culmination and its collapse.

As the viewer responds to the opening series of reflections upon which the film depends, she may be placed in a position partially analogous to that of the viewer of Hitchcock's *Vertigo* (1958). *Vertigo* makes the viewer continually question who is watching whom, whose actions are true and whose are false. Yet, minor discrepancies apart, Kim Novak's free fall at the end appears fairly definitive. The viewer's vertigo is by no means cured, I think, but the actuality of the second fall does not remain in doubt. Véronique, contrarily, does not follow her double's fate: she follows instead a *ligne de fuite* which leads her back to her father's house.

What this return might mean is perplexing for the viewer. Our puzzlement is by no means aided by Kieślowski's projected multiple endings, and two actual different endings of the film.[35] In the French print, Véronique returns to her father's house but does not yet go in.

The film finishes with a close-up of her hand, a white silhouette on the bark of a tree. In the print distributed in the USA, she goes into her father's house and is reunited and seemingly reconciled with him. Neither ending is more valid, I think; it is specifically their coexistence and difference which is important. Even in the ending of the film the viewer is denied definite proof. And in this sense Kieślowski's film may be closer than one might expect to the contemporary unravelling of visual evidence found in films such as *The Usual Suspects* (1994) where again we are brought to realize that all is virtual, and our sifting of visual evidence as viewers has been entirely deluded.

In interpreting the ending of *La Double Vie de Véronique*, I would argue that Véronique's return to the father's house is of little significance in this particular film. Her return works instead to prefigure Irène Jacob's reappearance in Kieślowski's filmmaking, specifically in *Rouge*. In this film, Valentine, played by Jacob, lives out a paternal/filial relation with the Judge she visits. Visual echoes, and the *mise-en-scène* Kieślowski deploys, work to link the Judge's house to the father's house. Where I have argued that *La Double Vie de Véronique* is anticipated by *Decalogue*, it in turn looks forward to the trilogy and allows the latter set of films to be known always already (but perhaps unconsciously) on a first viewing. Does the viewer of *Trois Couleurs: Bleu* realize immediately, for example, that a theme from the *Concert pour l'Unification de l'Europe* has already been heard in *La Double Vie de Véronique*? Images and actions also are repeatedly recalled. Véronique, for example, seeing the image of her double for the first time, approaches her finger to the photo and we see both image and finger in close-up. This tactile attention is viewed again in *Bleu* as Julie watches her daughter's funeral on the small television screen Olivier has placed beside her. There is, in a sense, interference between both the *mise-en-scène* and the meaning of the shots of the different films.

This linking device is rendered all the more evident in a repeated motif found in all four films. In *La Double Vie de Véronique*, Weronika, dressed only in her underwear, watches an old woman with heavy shopping from her window. Improbably she cries out that she is going to help her. We do not see whether this happens here: the scene appears to relate again, and instead, to the trilogy where, when each of the three protagonists encounters a figure bent over with bags, intent on putting a bottle in a bottle bank, it is only Valentine, in

Rouge, who will help her. Such links are rendered overt when pointed out, and there is a risk that Kieślowski's cinema appears to be entirely artificial, at best playful and at worst heavily contrived.

It seems unusual, then, that critics should write so forcefully of the emotion of his films, when everything seems to suggest that Kieślowski has, like Rohmer, abandoned emotion for thought. Critics often account for this emotion by discussing the sensitivity of Jacob's acting. For Romney: 'the film might seem a fairly conventional box of ontological tricks, recycling traditional metafictional paradoxes. But it offers enough texture and energy to escape the formalist bounds it ostensibly sets itself. Irène Jacob's performance is crucial in this respect, for it completely resists her integration into the film as mere cipher; this is all the more impressive since her part is essentially a function, duality personified.'[36] What this leaves aside is the way in which doubling itself, and such formalist play, may specifically provoke an emotional response.

Following Freud on the uncanny, the exploration of resemblance, indeterminacy and hesitation between actual and virtual might be clarified, in one sense at least. Freud, explaining uncanny familiarity, writes: 'There is a joking saying that "Love is homesickness"; and whenever a man dreams of a place or a country and says to himself, while he is still dreaming: "this place is familiar to me, I've been here before", we may interpret the place as being his mother's genitals or her body.'[37] Should the experience of wholeness in doubling relations of both Weronika and Véronique be compared to this phantasmatic return to intrauterine existence? The film provides us with the evidence that both women have lost their mothers at an early age: the identification with each other, the experience of mirroring and symbiosis thus could be explained, in simply Freudian terms, as the product of the desire to return to the maternal body and to know that place again. Such a reading, whilst efficient, serves the double purpose of rendering the experience the film projects pathological, on the one hand, and yet common, explicable, on the other.

Deleuze's refutations of the familial interpretations of psycho-analysis, explored in dialogue with Guattari, are well known. And it is partly as a result of this dismissal of singular interpretation and stable evidence that I have found Deleuze's work useful and illuminating for the purpose of interpreting Kieślowski's cinema. But here, I would suggest that links can be forged between Deleuze's work with Guattari and his later two-volume examination of cinema.

An examination of Kieślowski's cinema, and of *La Double Vie de Véronique* in particular, may work to reveal that the progeny of the time image, in postmodern cinema, is an 'image-hommage' which is purely virtual, and which leads the viewer into a non-curative and proliferating cinema of psychosis. Kieślowski's cinema is often spoken of in terms of mystery and mysticism. These terms become all too convenient labels for a cinema which places the viewer in a position to explore psychic disorder. A film such as *La Double Vie de Véronique* appears to confirm a series of paranoid fantasies about intuition, doubling and interconnection. The viewer herself is, ideally, the dupe of these paranoid fantasies. The film's betrayal comes as the viewer perceives that there will be no realization or actualization of the uncanny relations she has sensed. The doublings and allusions, the series of recognitions upon which the film depends, seem so many instances where our perception and comprehension are confirmed, where links offer pleasure to the viewer and offer her an illusion of mastery. The ultimate sense that our endeavour is in vain, however, and that this film is an exercise in representation and betrayal, is particularly unsettling. Even the *sujet supposé savoir* Kieślowski himself, suggests that his project was an aleatory one. He writes in the introduction to the English-language edition of *Decalogue*: 'we know no more than you. But maybe it is worth investigating the unknown, if only because the very feeling of not knowing is a painful one.'[38]

In Kieślowski's cinema, chance itself, and its hopeful ordering in the mind's eye of the viewer, becomes the organizing principle of individual films. Where Kieślowski seems to refute the logic and teleology of psychoanalytic interpretations, he nevertheless allows a complete pathology of misperception to enter into his exploration of the time-image (or its progeny) and of the viewer's response to such films. Kieślowski examines the full dissociative and disruptive effects of the indiscernibility of actual and virtual and represents these in Véronique's confusion and distress, which may in turn be recognized by the viewer. In this sense Kieślowski goes beyond Deleuze in showing how postmodern cinema projects, not a truth about time in the Bergsonian sense, but a series of fictions about time, illusion and identity, which remain themselves only ever virtual and ephemeral.

La Double Vie de Véronique allows us to think cinema differently and to think our relation to cinema differently. Kieślowski reveals the divorce between virtual and actual. In this sense it is fitting that in a film about France and Poland, if such this is, virtual France and virtual

Poland resemble each other, and cinematic and artistic representations of each other, more properly than they resemble either of their actual referents. Kieślowski's success is in creating scenes in another country, in another language, which are nevertheless always already familiar to viewers of his films. In *La Double Vie de Véronique*, Kieślowski makes a bilingual film which perpetually puts into question binary relations and the notion of difference. His entry into French cinema doubles his Polish cinema and reminds us that cinematic images embody their own difference, knowing only a virtual, and thus treacherous, relation to reality.

Notes to Chapter 1

1. Gilles Deleuze and Claire Parnet, *Dialogues* (Paris, 1996), 10, 11.
2. As Tony Rayns has argued, this film 'takes the constraints that have scuttled countless earlier movies (the need to balance different national interests, languages and cultures) and makes them the foundation of the fiction itself'. 'Kieślowski crossing over', *Sight and Sound* 1/11 (Mar. 1992), 22–3, 22.
3. Jean-Luc Douin, *Wajda* (Paris, 1981), 34, 31. An irony is that Wajda made *Danton* in France in 1982, the year following this interview.
4. Vincent Amiel, *Kieślowski* (Paris, 1995), 13.
5. A Polish article argues that *Decalogue* takes place in a world that does not exist: 'It is inhabited by doctors, artists, intellectuals of whose work we do not know anything and who do not have any financial worries.' Zygmunt Kałużyński, 'Technology shakes culture: cinema is dying, cinema is blooming', *Polityka* 10 (8 Mar. 1997), 50–3, 52 (in Polish). (I am very grateful to Dorota Ostrowska for drawing this to my attention and for translating the article for me.)
6. Christopher Dunkley, 'Rules for Life, Polish Style', *Financial Times* (13 June 1990), 17.
7. See Frank Leslie Cross, *The Oxford Dictionary of the Christian Church* (Oxford, 1983), 318–19, for discussion of the ordering of the Commandments in the various churches.
8. Paul Coates, 'The Curse of the Law: *The Decalogue*', in *Lucid Dreams: The Films of Krzysztof Kieślowski*, ed. P. Coates (Trowbridge, 1999), 94–115, 113 n.
9. Véronique Campan, *Dix brèves histoires d'image* (Paris, 1993), 15, 15.
10. Amiel, *Kieślowski*, 84.
11. Paul Coates, *The Story of the Lost Reflection: The Alienation of the Image in Western and Polish Cinema* (London, 1985), 44.
12. Amiel, *Kieślowski*, 19, 19–20.
13. Gilles Deleuze, *Cinéma 2: L'Image-temps* (Paris, 1985), 110, 110, 92, 94, 94, 94–5, 95, 95. D. N. Rodowick's *Deleuze's Time Machine* (Durham, NC, 1997) offers an illuminating and trenchant discussion of Deleuze's work on cinema and its context in the broader scheme of Deleuze's thinking.
14. Sigmund Freud, 'The "Uncanny"', *Penguin Freud Library 14. Art and Literature* (London, 1985), 335–76, 367, 367.

15. One of the most interesting studies which have appeared in this area, and one which offers a historical perspective on theories of spectatorship as well as a specific advance in thinking in this area, is the selection of essays edited by Linda Williams, *Viewing Positions: Ways of Seeing Film* (New Brunswick, NJ, 1995).
16. Rodowick, *Gilles Deleuze's Time-Machine*, p. xiv.
17. This concept is variously addressed in psychoanalytic film theory. See particularly Christian Metz, *Psychoanalysis and Cinema: The Imaginary Signifier* (London, 1982).
18. These images are effectively copied in the parting shots of Zhang Yimou's *Shanghai Triad* (1995).
19. As Kieślowski points out, there are only the most minor differences between the images of Irène Jacob as Weronika and as Véronique: 'Dans la partie française, elle a les cheveux plus courts de cinq centimètres environ. Pour moi, il était clair qu'elles devaient être toutes les deux semblables.' Michel Ciment and Hubert Niogret, 'De Weronika à Véronique', *Positif* 364 (June 1991), 26–31, 31. (Using Jeremy Irons to play a pair of identical twins in *Dead Ringers*, David Cronenberg took great care to bring out visual differences between the two sets of images of one actor.)
20. In this moment of death, Kieślowski alludes to the death of the character played by Janet Leigh in *Psycho* (1960).
21. Notably Žižek alluded to this particular scene in his lecture 'Women and their vicissitudes', given at the Museum of the Moving Image in London (June 1998).
22. Marcel Proust, *A la recherche du temps perdu*, I (Paris, 1954), 40.
23. The relevance of Proust to this Deleuzian reading of Kieślowski is by no means coincidental. Deleuze in his commentary on Bergson, and with specific reference to the 'image-cristal', writes: 'Dans le roman, c'est Proust qui saura dire que le temps ne nous est pas intérieur, mais nous intérieurs au temps qui se dédouble, qui se perd lui-même, qui fait passer le présent et conserver le passé.' Deleuze, *Cinéma 2*, 110. John Orr criticizes Deleuze, saying: 'his view of the modern as pure "time-image" which incorporates space is also profoundly Francocentric, a search for straight lineage from Bergson and Proust to Resnais and Robbe-Grillet.' *Cinema and Modernity* (Cambridge, 1993), 99. This criticism seems just, and may also reveal why Deleuze's work on cinema has proved an effective tool for analysing the French films of Kieślowski, who has worked precisely to adopt and adapt to the tradition of which Orr speaks, or indeed to show how elements of this tradition were always already present in his films.
24. The film was marketed as a 'thriller métaphysique'. *Film Français* acknowledges that Leonardo de la Fuente, the producer, was taking a risk with *La Double Vie de Véronique*. He is quoted accounting for the film's success in the following terms: 'Aujourd'hui les jeunes ne peuvent se raccrocher à aucune idéologie. Ils sont donc fascinés par les problèmes de l'au-delà, en dehors de toute connotation religieuse, des mondes parallèles, etc. C'est ce qui les a attirés dans *La Double Vie de Véronique* et que je n'avais pas prévu; d'une certaine façon ce film est lié à *Ghost* ou *Flatliners*.' Marie-Claire Arbaudie, 'Leonardo de la Fuente: Une législation inadéquate', *Film français* 2373 (25 Oct. 1991), 6.
25. Rayns, 'Kieślowski crossing over', 22.
26. Jonathan Romney, '*The Double Life of Véronique*', *Sight and Sound* 1/11 (Mar. 1992), 42–3, 43.

27. Ciment and Niogret, 'De Weronika à Véronique', 26.

28. Alain Masson, 'Subjectivité et singularité: *La Double Vie de Véronique*', *Positif* 364 (June 1991), 24–5, 24.

29. John Kim, 'Poles Apart 1: Krzysztof Kieślowski', *Columbia Film Review* 10/1 (1992), 2–5 and 39, 39, 39.

30. Ciment and Niogret, 'De Weronika à Véronique', 28.

31. Vincent Amiel draws different, but relevant parallels between *Ma Nuit chez Maud* and *Decalogue 3: Kieślowski*, 98. Geoff Andrew makes a useful, more general comparison between Kieślowski and Rohmer: *The 'Three Colours' Trilogy* (London, 1998), 80.

32. Freud, 'The "Uncanny"', 347.

33. Deleuze, *Cinéma 2*, 232, 232, 232, 233, 233.

34. Interestingly, Kieślowski's compatriot Agnieszka Holland uses Irène Jacob to play twin sisters, the mothers of Mary Lennox and her cousin Colin, in her adaptation of Frances Hodgson Burnett's novel, *The Secret Garden* (1994). The theme of doubling, uncanny resemblance and mistaken identity marks out Holland's work, most notably in *Olivier, Olivier* (1992).

35. For further discussion of this, see Annette Insdorf, *Double Lives, Second Chances: The Cinema of Krzysztof Kieślowski* (New York), 1999, 135.

36. Romney, '*The Double Life of Véronique*', 43.

37. Freud, 'The "Uncanny"', 368.

38. Krzysztof Kieślowski, *Decalogue: The Ten Commandments* (London, 1991), p. xiv.

CHAPTER 2

❖

Amnesia and the Time-Image
Trois Couleurs: Bleu

1 Recognitions

In *Trois Couleurs: Bleu* there is a brief scene where Julie, the film's protagonist, played by Juliette Binoche, goes to visit her mother in a *maison de retraite*. The scene opens with a long shot of Julie walking into the lush greenery of the institution grounds, emerging into the enclosed circle of her mother's world. The sterility and stillness of the institution, the dominant colours, white and green, of the scene, recall episodes early in the film where Julie herself is a patient, in a hospital or asylum where she is nursed after a car crash in which she loses her husband and small daughter. These links, visual and spatial, are, I will argue in what follows, of specific significance to our understanding of the mapping of memory and survival in *Bleu*.

The film cuts quickly from the institution grounds to the interior of the *maison de retraite* and a close-up of a photo frame which encloses several images: a smiling girl with long hair, a child and a sepia photo of a wedding. The camera moves steadily over these images leaving us time to search out resemblances. Within the wedding photo we see another image reflected. This is our first view of Julie's mother. It is necessarily virtual as we see her reflection in glass. The camera pulls the reflection, rather than the photo, into focus and leads us to see Julie reflected too, her face already framed as she looks in through a pane of glass in French windows. The film plays with reflection and virtual images on several levels, allowing the photographs (visual memory traces) to be overlaid by reflected images of a scene of (mis)recognition between mother and daughter.

This scene is indeed one of both recognition and misrecognition. The film works to establish the relations between the two women. We are treated to conventional shot/reverse shot editing as Julie speaks the word 'Maman...'[1] and looks at her mother who replies 'Marie-France...'. Julie must correct her mother and state her own identity, saying 'C'est moi, Julie'; she must work to remind her mother of her own presence. This drama of misrecognition is crucial to our understanding of Julie's position and trauma in the film. But equally important is the drama of recognition upon which this scene also depends, and which involves the spectator specifically, rather than the film's protagonists.

Julie's mother is played by Emmanuelle Riva: her face, seen so frequently in close-up in *Hiroshima mon amour*, is entirely recognizable, if a little thinner and more haunted. The appearance of Riva links *Bleu* to a particular generation of French cinema (just as the image of Binoche effectively links the film to contemporary productions). More than this, Riva allows Kieślowski to signal, I think, how far *Bleu* will pursue the examination of memory, and specifically memory loss, undertaken by Resnais and Duras in *Hiroshima mon amour*.

I have argued elsewhere that the trauma of *Hiroshima mon amour* is not the necessity of memory, but the possibility of forgetting.[2] Duras in her screenplay appears to testify to the pain of survival which depends on the loss of the past, the loss of memory, obliteration and forgetting. This is how the film will be remembered in *Bleu*; to perceive this it may be cogent to linger a moment over the source film and its memory narrative. Resnais's images in the first section of *Hiroshima mon amour* work crucially to recall and restore public memories of Hiroshima, and the horror of the atom bomb, yet the film's insistent dialogue reiterates the impossibility of witnessing or viewing such agony and suffering. As the tensions of the film are mapped onto a different scale in the retelling of the love affair at Nevers, and its partial repetition in the affair at Hiroshima, again *Hiroshima mon amour* seems to testify to the failure of memory and the artifice of representation, be it in a lovers' dialogue or in the words and images of a film. For the female protagonist, forgetting seems to bring little solace but only horror at the loss of memory traces which have allowed her to remain present in her own past history. This is exemplified late in the film. After she has spoken of her affair to her Japanese lover, she is seen speaking in the mirror of her hotel room to herself and to her mental image of the German soldier:

Tu n'étais pas tout à fait mort.
J'ai raconté notre histore.

Je t'ai trompé ce soir avec cet inconnu.
J'ai raconté notre histoire.
Elle était, vois-tu, racontable.
Quatorze ans que je n'avais pas retrouvé... le goût d'un amour impossible.
Depuis Nevers.
Regarde comme je t'oublie...
—Regarde comme je t'ai oublié.
Regarde-moi[3]

These words, which lament betrayal in a placing of past experience in present language, in a lack of recollection, are themselves repeated and reiterated at the very end of the film, as its narrative of desire comes full circle and the woman says now to her Japanese lover: 'Je t'oublierai! Je t'oublie déjà! Regarde comme je t'oublie! Regarde-moi!' The protagonist seems to experience, in Deleuzian terms, a break between the 'présent qui passe' and the memory of it which is constructed at the same moment. Resnais and Duras appear here to question the recording mechanisms of the human mind and to show how, *in extremis*, the present moment may be shattered by the awareness of its future absence.

If *Hiroshima mon amour* is a film primarily about memory loss and the pain of forgetting, my question here is how and why it is remembered in *Bleu*. The film is recalled literally and visually at several junctures. After Julie has made love with Olivier in the house she has steadily emptied, she leaves in the early morning and is seen walking alongside a stone wall and deliberately grazing her knuckles against the stones. Her bleeding hand, and the attempt to drown mental torment in physical pain, remind us necessarily of the female protagonist in *Hiroshima mon amour* who, locked in her parents' home after the loss of her German lover, cuts her hands repeatedly as she scrapes them against the cellar walls.[4]

Further, the images of lovers behind glass in *Bleu*, lovers slowly turning, their limbs entwined, recall the famous opening scenes of *Hiroshima mon amour* where the bodies of the Frenchwoman and her lover are seen as they make love. Indeed it is not only the visual resemblance between these scenes which is important: this is apparent but not entirely striking. Rather the similarity lies in the ways in which both films create a *mise-en-abyme* of their internal affective and visual drama. In both cases the bodies we see, and the acts of love they perform, are not shot in realist terms. In *Hiroshima mon amour* Resnais cuts between images of gleaming radioactive dust falling on the lovers, and images of the same bodies equally illumined by the sweat which glistens on their skin. The imbrication of Eros and Thanatos upon which the film depends is first established visually. These bodies are a compulsive point of return in the editing of the first sequences of the film, as Resnais begins to establish a frame of reference for the documentary shots of Hiroshima (both in the immediate aftermath of the bomb, and fourteen years later) which make up the memorable prelude to the love story which later unfolds. These shots of the lovers exist as metonym, then, which functions both as a part of the film, and as a sequence of images which sums up the film's themes and makes them visible and legible to the viewer.

The images of Julie and Olivier making love behind glass function similarly to frame the central concerns of *Bleu*. Kieślowski shoots an erotic scene which is asphyxiating, an image of return to a prior state: the lovers appear as if in a human aquarium, or in amniotic fluid. Their limbs are blanched and colourless, Julie's face presses against the glass which holds and frames them. The scene works to identify *Bleu* as a film of oblivion, of the drowning of memory, and of resurfacing and rebirth. If *Bleu* is a film about forgetting, it works, like *Hiroshima mon amour*, to explore this theme on a structural and visual level, effectively drawing into question once again the status of the time-image as defined by Deleuze. Indeed, as we have seen in analysis of *La Double Vie de Véronique*, the placing of images behind or in glass in Kieślowski's cinema (as in the aquarium scene in *Bleu*) serves to highlight the self-reflexivity of his films, their self-conscious representation of the visual and the act of viewing through a lens. In this way in *Bleu* Kieślowski explores the possibility of creating an 'image-hommage', a homage to Resnais, yet a set of images which explore the very impossibility of memory in the visual medium.

II Deleuze and Amnesia

How does *Bleu* look anew at memory, amnesia and the time-image? In *Cinéma 2: L'Image-temps* Deleuze explores and makes reference to questions of amnesia and memory disturbance in cinema. He seeks to explain why European cinema has taken as subject 'un ensemble de phénomènes, amnésie, hypnose, hallucination, délire, vision des mourants, et surtout cauchemar et rêve'.[5] He shows how these phenomena were an important aspect of Soviet cinema, and of German Expressionism, particularly in its links with psychiatry and psychoanalysis. In French cinema this interest is manifested in links with Surrealism. Deleuze explains that 'Le cinéma européen y voyait un moyen de rompre avec les limites "américaines" de l'image-action, et aussi d'atteindre à un mystère du temps, d'unir l'image, la pensée et la caméra dans une même "subjectivité automatique" par opposition à la conception trop objective des Américains'. For Deleuze, memory disturbance—'les troubles de la mémoire et les échecs de la reconnaissance'—works in cinema to provoke the correlation and confusion of actual and virtual: the 'image-souvenir' becomes effectively indissociable from the 'image-rêve' and the 'fantasme' as the relation between memory and fantasy is broken down. He looks at films such as Fellini's *8½*, René Clair's *Entr'acte* and Buñuel's *Un Chien andalou* in these terms. Yet the remainder of the chapter in *Cinéma 2: L'Image-temps*, 'Du souvenir aux rêves', moves off into exploration of musical comedy, and amnesia itself is passed over as a result. Deleuze mentions briefly in a footnote, however, that 'le cinéma soviétique affrontait les états de rêve (Eisenstein, Dovjenko...) mais aussi des états pathologiques du type amnésie, avec reconstitution de lambeaux de souvenirs'. It is precisely the question of these pathological states, these shreds of memory and their presence, and absences, in cinema, which will be explored further in this study of *Bleu*.

It seems correct to note that Deleuze's interest in memory disturbance relates primarily to the transformation of memory rather than its obliteration. In his reading of Resnais in particular he raises the specific question of 'l'oubli'. He argues, for example, with reference to Resnais: 'Il n'y a pas d'auteur moins enfoui dans le passé. C'est un cinéma qui, à force d'esquiver le présent, empêche le passé de se dégrader en souvenir. Chaque nappe de passé, chaque âge sollicite à la fois toutes les fonctions mentales: le souvenir mais aussi l'oubli, le faux souvenir, l'imagination, le projet, le jugement...'. Deleuze's account here fails to explore the question of the betrayal of the past in memory traces. This reflects his interest in the state and status of the image, as opposed to the issue of the impression it produces in the mind of the spectator. Deleuze views *Hiroshima mon amour* as a film which moves into a new space of the future, a new mapping of self, place and present. He writes: 'C'est comme deux régions de passé incommensurables, Hiroshima, Nevers. Et tandis que le Japonais refuse que la femme entre dans sa propre région [...], la femme attire dans la sienne le Japonais volontaire et consentant, jusqu'à un certain point. N'est-ce pas pour chacun une manière d'oublier sa propre mémoire, et de se faire une mémoire à deux, comme si la mémoire maintenant devenait monde et se détachait de leurs personnes?' Although it passes without comment, it appears that Deleuze approves this escape from subjective memory, this new propulsion into the future. There is little space for regret in his account. Yet in *Hiroshima mon amour*, betrayal and its attendant horrors are, as I have argued, noticeably more insistent.

This refusal of regret is symptomatic of Deleuze's work in *Cinéma 2: L'Image-temps*. More generally, his account of memory disturbance in cinema does not explore the affective dimension of (the representation of) pathological states. For Deleuze exploring memory, it seems that loss itself is not an issue. The case is very different for the protagonists I am discussing and, perhaps, for the viewer as well. Indeed, in representations of amnesia, memory disturbance and forgetting, films may be seen to question the role of the viewer and the possible analytic function of viewing. This assertion may lead us to a series of questions about the ways in which filmmakers may give themselves, and their spectators, privileges over the traumatized or amnesiac protagonist. I would ask how far the spectator's involvement, her judgement of time and memory relations in a film, and even her memory (and forgetting) of images and scenes in a film are implicated in a film's presentation of the time-image. It seems that similar questions are already raised in the cinema of Alain Resnais, and pursued further in Kieślowski's partial homage to Resnais in *Bleu*. However, a distinction must yet be made here. Resnais notably makes the complicit viewer party to his characters' subjective visions: we see the drama of Nevers in *Hiroshima mon amour*, yet remain uncertain whether the images we see constitute literal flashback, the distorted memories of the Frenchwoman, her fantasies of her past life, or the Japanese man's fantasies inspired by the Frenchwoman's narration. Kieślowski, contrarily, refuses flashback or 'images-souvenir' in *Bleu*. Instead he makes his viewers share Julie's trauma by denying vision altogether and placing the very 'trous de mémoire' we assume his protagonist experiences in the structure of the film. In this sense Kieślowski, like Resnais, explores an essentially pathological state but questions further the capacity of the time-image to represent the very absence of memory. The viewer shares the protagonist's lapses of memory as Kieślowski attempts to re-think the cinematic representation of trauma.

III Julie

Julie is the psychic subject of *Bleu*. She plays the role of Riva in *Hiroshima mon amour*, but in a new time dimension and transformed cinematic medium. *Bleu* depends on its own series of repetitions and displacements, and it is in these terms that it is both revealing and unsettling to re-think the links that are established in the film between Julie herself and her amnesiac mother. Where Riva, in *Hiroshima mon amour*, plays a character who bemoans the necessity and pain of forgetting, Kieślowski casts her in *Bleu* as a woman whose very faculties appear annihilated and who seems to be becoming slowly enclosed in her own world of absence. This is signalled overtly in the coda to the film, in a sequence of images which follows the scene where Julie and Olivier make love behind glass. The images unfold in accordance with the music from the now completed *Concert pour l'Unification de l'Europe*. The words which have been set to music here form the familiar passage from St Paul's Letter to the Corinthians. An image of Julie's mother briefly comes into focus: she is again seen first as a set of reflections and only latterly as an actual figure, before she closes her eyes and the image shifts into blackness. The words which accompany these images come, all too aptly, from the lines: 'car les prophéties prendront fin,/les langues se tairont,/la connaissance disparaître'.[6] It is with these words that Kieślowski frames his representation of Julie's mother, and we find ourselves specifically aware of the function she holds in the film.

One fear of the film lies, I think, despite its seemingly exultant ending, in the proximity between Julie's experiences of cutting herself off from her past and those of her mother. Here we return to the scene I have analysed at the start of the chapter. What is disturbing in fact is, despite her confusion, the very relevance of the mother's comments to Julie's identity and place in the film. Indeed the scene of misrecognition between the protagonists is slowly revealed to hold recognizable significance for the viewer in the course of the film.

We might consider, for example, how we account for the fact that Julie's mother appears not to recognize her. This appears, on one level, a literal result of the mother's amnesia and confusion. Yet it is true, too, that by this stage in the film Julie has, both involuntarily and deliberately, severed her links with the past and created a new identity for herself. In some senses, in the film, this itself is recognized, as the mother does not see the daughter as herself. Following this line of argument further, we might say that it is also significant that the mother misrecognizes her daughter as Marie-France. These are the words with which the mother greets the daughter, and this is the delusion which repeatedly surfaces through the scene, despite Julie's reminders to her mother of her own identity, *and* the mother's seeming acceptance of these.

Recognizing Julie as Marie-France, the mother says: 'Ils m'avaient dit que tu étais morte.' She adds, in confusion: 'Tu as l'air bien.' The mother's sister, Marie-France, is indeed dead, as we learn, and on one level this accounts for the mother's delusion. Yet her words to Julie in the context of the film again, I think, speak something of the truth of Julie's condition and identity. It is possible to conjecture that the car crash itself is a near-death experience: it constitutes the erasure of Julie's family, her husband, her child, her position in that family. As Julie comes back into consciousness in the hospital (in a scene I shall look at in more detail below), memories of the event seem to be absent, her waking takes the form of a re-birth or resurrection. In the hospital itself she makes a suicide attempt, further attempting, it might be argued, to actualize the virtual death she has experienced. The fact that Julie looks fine, that she is in fact surviving, may itself surprise the viewer as much as Julie's mother. Her mother seems to recognize, unthinkingly, Julie's status here as *revenant*.

The possibility that the mother ever recognizes Julie during this scene remains constantly in the balance. Julie is called to demonstrate her identity again, saying: 'Mais je ne suis pas ta sœur, maman. Je suis ta fille.' Where the mother again seems to accept this fact, the effect of the scene lies in its evocation of constant amnesia, of the obliteration of short-term memory: in a Durassian sense, lacunae develop between statements. No continuity of knowledge, memory or identity is allowed to develop. Like a character in Duras, the mother asks her daughter to tell her something of her life: she will only attempt to know her daughter's life as a narrative. Julie herself engages in this desire and chooses, like the Frenchwoman in Hiroshima, the fact of her trauma as the narrative of her identity. She says in the film (but not the script): 'J'ai perdu mon mari et mon enfant...'. For the first time in the film, Julie is shown to find words to describe her experience; yet they seem oddly clipped and devoid of emotion. Further, her mother proves an inadequate witness to Julie's testimony: she claims knowledge of the events which have disrupted her daughter's memory and identity, saying that she has been told, yet offers no emotion or response, and physically turns away from her daughter. When Julie asks: 'Maman, tu m'écoutes?',[8] her mother replies: 'Je t'écoute, Marie-France.' It seems that Julie is perpetually displaced in her mother's memory, her position unfixed.

Aptly, again, this scene provides the moment in the film when Julie will give words to her newly constructed relation to the past. She tells her mother: 'Je ne veux plus de possessions, plus de souvenirs.' We have previously seen Julie stripping her life of possessions and material reminders of the past. Are these the 'souvenirs' she speaks of or does she refer also to mental images, to the possible resurrection of the past in the present which memory provides? In these terms the viewer is left in doubt as to how far Julie's amnesia is voluntary or unwilled. Does she deliberately evacuate any memory traces in order to deny their partial or disturbed state? Again, an irony of this scene lies in the fact that Julie appears to come to see her amnesiac mother in order to seek out a memory of herself as a child. Having been horrified by the mice in her new apartment, she comes to ask her mother whether she was afraid of mice as a child. Her mother replies: 'C'est Julie qui avait peur.' A divide is created between the Julie who is present as an adult who is unable to communicate with her mother, and the fearful child Julie, whose photo we have perhaps seen in the frame at the start of the scene and whose presence in the mother's memory appears to have eradicated the existence of her daughter in her mind in the present. Again she turns her head away and again Julie comes to experience her own identity as other, as other in the mind of her mother.

But the severance from the mother is not as fearful as the connections to her which this scene establishes. As Julie approaches at the start of the scene we see that her mother is watching television. She seems to be entirely intent on watching images which imitate a free fall, which show a figure jumping into oblivion, hanging from a thread. The soundtrack of the programme imitates circus music and the scene appears to offer a televisual and exterior equivalent of the images of a highwire artist found in Kafka or Klima. As Julie's mother watches the television she says: 'On voit le monde entier.' As televisual images are used in Kieślowski the statement is patently not true and here the link between Julie and her mother may begin to emerge.

IV Television

Televisual images appear fairly frequently in Kieślowski's films: the television screen becomes a further surface for the projection and reflection of virtual images.[9] What is significant, indeed, about Kieślowski's use of the televisual image is the way in which it is used not to bring the outside world into the frame of his *intimiste* filmmaking, but in fact to make the inner world of his protagonists' psyche, memory and identities visible to the viewer. I find this the only way to account for the fact that Kieślowski's characters, as television viewers, insistently find dramas of their own lives reflected quite literally on the screen, as if by chance. This will be seen to be entirely significant when I look at *Rouge* in my last chapter, but already in *Bleu*, psychic interference and self-visualization seem inherent in Kieślowski's use of the television screen.

In *Bleu*, Julie only watches television to see her own life. In the first instance Olivier brings a miniature screen to the hospital so that she can see the funeral of her husband and child. This first viewing of her life is conscious and deliberate, yet it initiates further unwilled interference between self and image. Like Véronique recognizing herself in her photographs from Kraków, Julie recognizes her grief in the televisual images and puts up her finger to touch the screen. She first sees the images which work to actualize her loss: the scene is extremely moving for both protagonist and viewer, in the pathos of the child's small coffin, and in Julie's mute, charged reaction. The television gives her an image of her loss, around which to construct her new, bereft identity. Yet we find too that as the funeral service continues Julie's grief overwhelms her power to act as viewer and to view her loss. She does not turn away from the screen or turn it off, instead the images themselves disappear as the screen goes out of focus and the scene is disrupted in interference. As her mind blanks out in denial, the televisual image, and our vision as spectators, is suddenly curtailed.

This sense of subjective vision is corroborated in a later scene where Julie is woken at night and goes to Lucille's stripjoint at her friend's request. In a neighbouring room, the television is on and a late-night arts programme is visible. Julie realizes that its subject is her husband Patrice and that she recognizes the images on the screen. The film plays between the plausible and the implausible. On the one hand this is a likely topic for such a programme, and its timing is entirely in accordance with French television schedules. But that this programme should be on, by chance, here, and that Julie should, by chance, see it, seems altogether more contrived. Indeed the emergence of the programme on the screen seems to act instead in accordance with the stage in her mourning which Julie has reached, and indeed the stage we have reached in the film we are viewing.

It is an irony of Kieślowski's cinema, then, that he should appear to reflect changes in technology and audio-visual representation, placing so many screens within the frames of his films (note the computer screen in *Decalogue 1*, the ultrasound screen in *Bleu*), yet these screens themselves offer so many inward reflections of the anguished protagonists who are the films' primary subject. Kieślowski appears to use mass communication for the contrary purpose of approaching yet more closely, and in more intimate detail, the psychic dramas and traumas of the individual. This, at least partially, is the case as we find it in *Bleu*. But where Kieślowski makes the individual his focus, in painful, hermetic detail, it should be recognized that his interest in *Bleu* is in exploring how her trauma remains invisible to her, how representation betrays rather than releases pain, and in addressing how the cinematic medium can respond to and reflect the very absences of the psychic subject.

In examining *Bleu* as a film about the loss of mental images, I have argued that it is concerned with links and parallels between Julie and her mother. This is revealed in televisual terms. As Olivier brings Julie the miniature television screen to see the funeral, he switches it on briefly and here we see almost indistinguishable images of flight and fall, of *vertige* and emptiness. These images later seem to be recalled as Julie's mother watches television in the *maison de retraite*: implicitly, I would argue, we find a contiguity between the mental pictures and psychic states of mother and daughter. They are both shown to be amnesiacs living out a willed or unwilled, partial and fractured relation to their own past.

v Survival and Denial

For Julie, survival is achieved in the denial of memories of her past. This is a problematic position to accept ethically, both in the film and for its viewer, yet the fact that *Bleu* raises problems like this confirms its status as an engaged analysis of the traumatized psyche. Kieślowski has been criticized (in a review of *Bleu*) for his 'blithe abandonment of social issues and retreat into a remote, mystical realm where personal experience is all that matters'.[10] The reviewer, considering Kieślowski's place in European filmmaking, suggests indeed that his concerns 'do not augur well for the future'. Such a critique of Kieślowski tends to rely on a notion of division between his 'socially engaged' Polish filmmaking and his aesthetic, solipsistic French productions. Yet to posit such a division is again inaccurate: despite proving an engaging (and engaged) critic and analyst of the state of Poland in the 1970s and 1980s, Kieślowski has always been concerned with the individual, or more precisely with the point of view a particular individual adopts and how this reflects or refracts the political and cultural dominants of his period. This is notably and self-consciously the case in a film such as *Camera Buff* or indeed *From a Night Porter's Point of View*. If anything, Kieślowski is interested in the paradox of a politics of vision, whereby the identity of the individual is constructed with relation to what they see, and yet what they see is a product of their own fantasies, delusions and point of view. (These are issues to which I shall return in the chapter on *Blanc*.) MacNab, criticizing Kieślowski and his scriptwriter Piesiewicz, continues: 'Their "unpolitical", almost Proustian project is to consider how far individuals are able to detach themselves from family, memory and material objects, the very things which give life definition.' Such an argument works to link Kieślowski specifically with a French strain of modernism. Such a lineage of influence would seem to suggest that Kieślowski's project is outdated in postmodernity, however inclined we might be to dispute the dismissive reading of the politics of Proust's own project. But I think the reading itself is at fault: little of Proust's concern with the imbrication of memory and identity survives in Kieślowski, despite (as I have argued in the previous chapter) the possible resemblances between their explorations of representation. Indeed the Proustian concern with the layering and possible redemption of the past, influenced by Bergson, and influencing Deleuze, seems precisely the object of Kieślowski's critique. Kieślowski is concerned in *Bleu* not with redemption of the past, but with a contingent survival in the present. Detachment from family, memory and material objects may be Kieślowski's subject in *Bleu*, but such an act of rupture is precipitated by trauma, and not the mere solipsistic will of the psychic subject.

Survival in the face of loss has long been a dominant theme in Kieślowski's filmmaking: the mourning and trauma which are the subject of *Bleu* find their precedents in *No End*, *Decalogue 1* and more subliminally in *La Double Vie de Véronique*. Where I have been arguing for a continuum in Kieślowski's filmmaking between Poland and France, and a constancy in preoccupation, some development in the exploration of specific themes can be witnessed, and this is the case particularly with the thematics of mourning. In *No End*, Urszula, played by Grażyna Szapołowska, loses her husband, is haunted by him and follows him to death. In *Decalogue 1*, Kieślowski leaves a father in the face of the full horror of his son's death: survival is rendered almost unthinkable. Survival will be thought through in *Bleu*.

Survival is one of the most charged issues of Kieślowski's filmmaking. It is Kieślowski's specific subject in *Decalogue 8* where he examines survival and responsibility in the context of the experiences of a teacher of ethics who encounters a figure, almost a *revenant*, from her past. In this film Kieślowski overtly indicates the inseparable links between the issue of (lack of) survival and the experience of deportation and the Holocaust. Perhaps survival and the experience of trauma must necessarily be re-thought in this context in the post-war era. And while, of course, Julie's trauma and survival as represented in *Bleu* have no relation to the Holocaust, and are perhaps essentially incomparable with the experience of Holocaust survivors, nevertheless studies of trauma and memory inspired and provoked by the experiences of Holocaust survivors will be of particular relevance to the exploration of psychic disturbance Kieślowski constructs in *Bleu*.

The trilogy is itself as a whole a meditation on the possibilities of survival. The end of the trilogy and its survival narrative (which I shall look at in more detail in the chapter on *Rouge*) have aroused both popular and critical interest. Kieślowski stages a ferry disaster of the proportions of the Zeebrugge disaster. The viewer discovers at the end of the trilogy that amongst the seven survivors of the disaster are the protagonists of the three films. This has been read as a heavily stylized, self-conscious happy ending; as evidence of Kieślowski's grotesque manipulation of public trauma for the purposes of personal filmmaking; and indeed as evidence of his authoritarian stance, playing God with his characters. The ethics of fictionalizing a real event apart, I would argue that the ending of the trilogy has been misread. Rather than providing an over-determined conclusion, the ending in fact stands as the very cause and reason behind telling the tales and viewing the lives of these seemingly unconnected protagonists. It is not so much that Kieślowski saves the protagonists in his film in an act of wish-fulfilment or divine grace in the ending of the trilogy; it is rather that the three separate tales are told only because they lead to this peculiar point of convergence. The blind chance of these protagonists' survival becomes the motivation for the filmic narration of each life history. The films are determined by their ending; in other words it is only in their ending that we can understand their origin and purpose. In this sense, in part, the teleology of viewing is disrupted. The fact that the end of the films is already known, on some levels, and that their events are pre-determined is overtly signalled and corroborated by the flashforwards which thread through *Blanc*. And indeed more generally in these films I would argue that Kieślowski encourages viewer and protagonists alike to look forwards and to refuse a backward glance (despite their sense of the lure of the past and its illusions).

Julie, in *Bleu*, is always already a survivor. Her place in the trilogy is dependent on her future survival, yet it is her recurring present which structures the film. Survival, and, in this particular instance, more literally physical survival in a car crash and psychical survival through denial and repression are the compelling features of the film. It is my aim, in the part of this chapter which remains, to work out how Kieślowski might be said to manipulate the filmic medium so that he may explore the denial of memory and the denial of response in images and sound. This investigation will involve further engagement with Deleuze, and also with theorists who have made testimony, survival and post-traumatic stress disorder the specific subject of their analysis. I want to think through further issues with relation to memory disturbance in cinema which Deleuze leaves largely untouched, and which have, arguably, arisen in post-Deleuzian film.

VI Past and Present

The survival of trauma can be seen to depend notionally on the construction of a relation between a self in the present and a self or selves in the past. Identity may depend on negotiating and controlling the relations between these selves, on constructing a historical sequence of personal identity and a realization of the primacy of the present. It is in these terms that we may perceive an important relation between Deleuze's work on time in the cinema, and the specific issue of the construction of identity in time and in survival. Deleuze's theory of cinema reveals how far the process of making sense through time, in time and of time, is an inherent property of the cinematic medium and a dimension of film that is foregrounded in the work of certain filmmakers (such as Resnais, whose importance in *Bleu* I am stressing, or Pasolini, on whom Deleuze will draw specifically).

Deleuze suggests that in cinema, in the first place, 'c'est le montage lui-même qui constitue le tout, et nous donne ainsi l'image *du* temps'.[11] He alludes to Pasolini, saying that 'le montage a la propriété de "rendre le présent passé", de transformer notre présent instable et incertain en "un passé clair, stable et descriptible", bref d'accomplir le temps'. For Deleuze, montage itself, the construction and arrangement of a series of filmic images, serves the purpose of fixing and integrating, of rendering significant. In this sense, in this construction of an image of time (rather than of a time-image) an individual shot is associated with the very tenuous certainty of present perception, where the sequence of shots constructs events from a retrospective stance which allows their meaning to be brought out in temporal and progressive terms.

This reading of the image of time in cinema, and analysis of the temporal function of editing or montage, is in keeping, I would argue, with an integrative, normative and curative view of identity where a stable relation exists between past and present. The interest here of Deleuze's work in *Cinéma 2: L'Image-temps* lies in his recognition that this is not entirely the experience of time as we know it: cinema has given a falsified image of time, but can come closer to representing time as it is lived in the development of the time-image itself. The transition from the image of time to the time-image is important. As Deleuze reminds us: 'Selon Pasolini, "le présent se transforme en passé", en vertu du montage, mais ce passé "apparaît toujours comme un présent", en vertu de la nature de l'image'. Each image in a film can be seen to be lived and presented as a present moment, despite the retrospective positioning and perspective constructed by the editor and experienced by the viewer. There is a tension, then, between the temporal perspective of montage and the ontology of the photographic image. The quality and the status of the photographic image may encourage the viewer to let an intimation of similarity and simultaneity undermine any absolute sense of teleology in temporal terms (and this is an aspect of film which Kieślowski himself consciously exploits, as I shall discuss further below). For Deleuze, this movement away from linear chronology is recognized in the self-conscious development of the time-image. The fixity of relations between past and present, established at least by editing, gives way to flux and effective overlayering of temporal sequences and associative relations. This appears the true (a)temporal potential of the medium.

Deleuze suggests, very forcefully: 'il n'y a pas de présent qui ne soit hanté d'un passé ou d'un futur, d'un passé qui ne se réduit pas à un ancien présent, d'un futur qui ne consiste pas en un présent à venir'. This reality of mental process can be reflected and represented in cinema. He claims indeed: 'Il appartient au cinéma de saisir ce passé et ce futur qui coexistent avec l'image présente. Filmer ce qui est *avant* et ce qui est *après*... Peut-être faut-il faire passer à l'intérieur du film ce qui est avant le film, et après le film, pour sortir de la chaîne des présents.' And even this desire to extend the cinematic representation of temporal relations beyond the present moment into the past remembered and imagined, and the future, projected and fantasized, is not enough for Deleuze. He speaks not merely of the span and implications of a film's subject in temporal terms, but also of the nature of the image itself, claiming for example that the aim of *cinéma-vérité* is 'non pas atteindre à un réel tel qu'il existerait indépendamment de l'image, mais atteindre à un avant et un après tels qu'ils coexistent avec l'image, tels qu'ils sont inséparables de l'image'.

The question becomes all the more complex if we consider that the time-image depends on a correlation between the experience of time of the protagonist of the film, the representation of temporality exploited and explored by the director, and the temporal experience of viewing where the spectator herself is responsible for perceiving, or indeed constructing, the relations between past, present and future which might be mapped in any single image. It is this correlation, I would argue, that Kieślowski tests in *Bleu*. In many ways Kieślowski can be seen to explore the time-image in Deleuze's terms. For Deleuze: 'Non seulement l'image est inséparable d'un avant et d'un après qui lui sont propres, qui ne se confondent pas avec les images précédentes et suivantes, mais d'autre part elle bascule elle-même dans un passé et dans un futur dont le présent n'est plus qu'une limite extrême, jamais donné.' Kieślowski's filmmaking, with its tacit links and inner reflections, makes us think through these relations of 'before' and 'after' specified by Deleuze; and in keeping with Deleuze's second statement, Kieślowski achieves too this very temporalization of the image, through an emphasis on duration and movement, however brief, in time within a particular shot. Put another way, Kieślowski's cinema demonstrates a recognition of the ways in which the time-image, which already holds its own relations of past, present and future, is also deepened and inflected by its relation in time to other images within the film.

As I have suggested, one major achievement of *Bleu* is its use of the time-image to question absence in memory and the refusal of temporal integration. Kieślowski draws us to wonder how a film may refuse or question temporal ordering and processing. *Bleu* is a film which explores the incommensurability of past trauma and present survival. *Bleu* works to testify to the refusal of memory, to survival in denial and in the deadening of response. This Kieślowski explores in terms of *mise-en-scène* and editing, and further through a dialectics of intimacy and distance which persuades us that the protagonist's trauma remains opaque to her. Ironically, then, Kieślowski makes use of editing and the enchainment of images to construct an image of time which is both disturbed and dissociated. And it is thus that the viewer experiences Julie's own memory disturbance.

In order to understand further the temporal dislocations and psychic disorder of *Bleu*, it may be helpful to consider recent work on trauma, survival and post-traumatic stress disorder. Post-traumatic stress disorder is considered collectively in a volume of essays edited by Cathy Caruth, who implicitly associates the traumatized response to bereavement, to abuse and to specifically life-threatening experiences. Julie's experience of bereavement as represented in *Bleu* falls easily within the scope of her discussion. Caruth's work is particularly interesting in its near spatial mapping of relations between trauma and memory. She speaks of traumatic nightmare as a 'space to which willed access is denied'.[12] She relates this notion of the denial of willed access specifically to amnesia and to the question of the flash-back which 'provides a form of recall that survives at the cost of willed memory'. The psychic subject is shown to be at once excluded from her memories, and incarcerated within the spaces of involuntary memory. The reappearance of unwilled memory defies logic and disrupts the subject's survival in the present: her relation to the present is always contingent, and dependent only on the present absence of the past recalled. Caruth suggests that 'the ability to recover the past is [...] closely and paradoxically tied up, in trauma, with the inability to have access to it'. I would suggest that this is the paradox with which Kieślowski contends in his filmic representation of trauma, and his re-viewing of the time-image.

It is perhaps significant that the term 'flashback' appears in both psychological discourse and film criticism, yet its meaning, in each case, is rather different. It is indeed crucial that in cinematic terms *Bleu* entirely refuses the use of flashback. The danger of presenting flashback (or the recurrence of visual memories) in film is that the viewer adopts the role which the traumatized survivor may not yet or ever be able to play. In these terms the viewer may seek to integrate the intrusive time sequence into an explanatory teleology within the filmic narrative. In general cinematic terms this might be seen as one of the very purposes of flashbacks which serve to explain the present, to cast light on their history, and to place the viewer in a position where she may understand the temporal and causal relations of the film more completely. As Maureen Turim observes in her study of flashbacks in film: 'Flashbacks traditionally give us a clear visual image of the past';[13] though she reminds us that 'one of the modernist impulses will be to throw this clarity of visualization of memory into question'.

In psychology, the symptom of post-traumatic stress disorder described as a flashback has still more disorienting properties and implications. Caruth suggests: 'The history that a flashback tells [...] is [...] a history that literally has no place, neither in the past, in which it was not fully experienced, nor in the present, in which its precise images are not fully understood.'[14] The flashback, in psychological terms, seems precisely to disrupt the temporalization of the image as theorized by Deleuze and to demonstrate an instance where images exist outside temporal teleology and psychic control. In *Bleu* Kieślowski presents a psychic subject who is prey to such symptoms of psychic disorder. Yet the filmmaker refuses to give the viewer access to the mental images of the psychic subject, thus placing us in a position where we are in part unable to integrate the temporal relations of the film. In *Bleu* no integration is effected; indeed, instead, survival depends on the denial of memory and identity, and the concomitant subsidence of the symptoms of trauma. To demonstrate this I want to look further at a scene from the film which serves to place both survivor and viewer in denial. The scene I have chosen begins immediately after the car crash in which Julie loses her husband, her daughter and her own identity.

vii Trauma

The scene after the car crash opens with an image which appears at first formless and meaningless: fibres on cloth. The camera lingers in extreme close-up on these and their perceptible movements. It becomes possible to work out, a few shots later, that this is fluff on Julie's pillow. Our first images derive entirely from Julie's point of view and angle of vision. The images are objective, yet the use of extreme close-up and the resulting insularity of vision persuade us that these images serve to indicate the status of Julie's subjectivity and the limits of her perception. But we do not remain within Julie's point of view: her subjective vision is then supplemented by another extreme close-up, this time of the pupil of her eye in whose convex and glistening surface we see reflected a doctor who speaks to Julie. We see now both what she sees and her eye looking. Her eye becomes the screen on which the doctor's image is projected: this indicates how far Kieślowski works to place the membrane of Julie's consciousness between the viewer and the events of the narration. Through this membrane, in this membrane, we will look at the world she perceives around her, and it is thus, rather than in the direct representation of mental images, that we will gain access to Julie's state of mind and its relation to both present and past. In this sense, whilst maintaining Julie constantly, almost obsessively within the gaze of the camera, the film itself is inflected at certain moments by her perceptions: as her mind blanks out, in denial, our vision also is suddenly curtailed.

The close-up image of Julie's eye may be taken to exemplify the time-image as studied by Deleuze. In the first place we are presented with a single take: the camera focuses on the eye for a number of seconds, holding it in suspension as the doctor's words follow one another in time. His words work on one level to map out past, present and future inexorably. The scene is one which exploits duration and a supposedly irreversible move from ignorance to knowledge. However brief the sequence, Kieślowski makes the viewer pause in the duration of suffering. His filmmaking fairly frequently has this effect of drawing out time, in silence, stillness and an inexorable focus on a single object. This is exemplified, for example, in the later shots where Julie watches her husband's and daughter's funeral. The camera follows the responses in her face, enacting its own denial of our vision as it closes in only on her mouth, demonstrating how far her pain can only be seen in parts, is inexpressible in its entirety. The use of metonymy here reveals an extreme economy in means of expression, and yet an awareness too of the ways in which the camera may work to enact the pathos and pain of mental disintegration in an intense focus on a specific body part. Julie is not whole but fractured here, and it is in these terms that she is seen by camera and viewer. As she supposedly hears of her trauma, as it is momentarily made present within her, we as viewers stare into her retina, and perceive both her extreme mental myopia and our extreme intimacy with her vision of events. Yet despite this intimacy we are left with an inescapable inability to know the other or to image or imagine her response. Kieślowski leaves the viewer in a position of doubt, and this is reflected even, and overtly, in temporal terms.

Where I have argued that the doctor's words may seem to map out the temporal relations of the hospital scene and its place within the film, in fact knowledge of time has been disrupted both by Julie's experience of trauma and, ironically, by Kieślowski's use of editing. After the car crash, viewed by the young boy in the field, the film's recording of events is abruptly interrupted. The film seems to lapse in Julie's unconsciousness, and to come only slowly into focus again as she comes to in the hospital. The viewer thus has no notion how long after the accident this awakening takes place; and the viewer will learn only with Julie the loss she has suffered. In effect, as viewers, we know only the absence of knowledge of the protagonist herself.

The doctor asks Julie whether she was conscious in the accident: he seeks to know whether she is aware of what has happened to her. The viewer is presented with the same question. In this scene Julie appears to have no knowledge of her trauma and to respond to it only here: this reaction certainly leads us to conjecture that this is her first discovery of her loss. Yet we encounter the possibility as well that what has been known has been denied. Is Julie, like her mother, constantly awakened into a consciousness of events? The absence in the film between the crash and Julie's awakening may be a space of unconsciousness, but may also be a space of amnesia. And, disquietingly, we will never as viewers enter this space, and thus know the location of Julie's trauma. We may see into its material analogues in the course of the film, but willed access to the space of trauma will always be denied. Again we are left with a film of hypothesis. This lack of spectatorial privilege is itself significant. Duras has stated, with much resonance: 'Tout ce qu'on peut faire c'est de parler de l'impossibilité de parler de HIROSHIMA',[15] and this intimation is reflected in the reminders of the impossibility of knowledge and witnessing which subtend *Hiroshima mon amour*. Kieślowski appears to demonstrate the same caution and the same refusal in his representation of trauma and mourning. *Bleu* is a film about the impossibility of seeing and re-

viewing the traumatic experience of the other. What it questions further is whether the protagonist herself will also gain access to her own memories of her past experience.

I would argue indeed that Kieślowski implicitly questions whether the doctor's words narrating her trauma to Julie can ever effectively be known (in the film or otherwise). Julie may literally not know what the doctor tells her as the camera gazes into her eye, but can she ever really know this trauma as the narrative of her own life? When Julie dismisses the journalist who attempts to invade her privacy and mourning to ask questions about her life and responses, Julie narrates her experience as if it is entirely exterior to her, as if she is not the 'I' who is the survivor of the events she describes. The same distancing in narrative is found as Julie speaks to her mother. This distance of Julie from herself has a direct impact on, or is reflected in, Kieślowski's manipulation of the image.

As I have said, Kieślowski denies us any direct vision of Julie's imagined or remembered internal images, or of the instances of flash-back she appears to experience. Instead her emotions are explored externally in both editing and *mise-en-scène*. This can be witnessed specifically in the scene which immediately follows Julie's encounter with the doctor. The film cuts to the breaking of a pane of glass: this functions familiarly as delayed reaction, as displaced image of Julie's internal response to her trauma. Yet it opens too into a new series of spatial metaphors, where the glass, the blank walls, the whiteness and vacancy of the clinic allow us to enter the new spaces of Julie's mind. Julie's environment appears the product of her consciousness: we are offered a privileged entrance into her state of mind spatially, rather than visually, in the projection of mental images. Yet this entrance affords only the knowledge that Julie herself is distanced from her memory, and her identity. Her mind is emptied out, as she will later literally strip the house where she lived with her husband and child of its furniture and her possessions.

In this use of spatial metaphor, Kieślowski again comes close to Resnais, who exploits the blankness yet expressivity of the spaces of the hotel, the hospital and the museum in Hiroshima. For Resnais, these are spaces where memory is attempted but proves inadequate, where lost objects and fractured lives cannot be repossessed and integrated. For Kieślowski, equally, spaces of trauma become the location of amnesia and forgetting.

VIII Involuntary Memory

Julie is the victim of sudden intrusions of traumatic recollection: this is first evidenced in a scene in the hospital where she jolts awake in response to music and the ethereal blue light with which Kieślowski chooses to replace any memory traces. The viewer is left here with the question whether, in music and light, the film offers a literal or metaphoric representation of these intrusions of memory. If this is literally Julie's experience of involuntary memory, it seems in keeping with the sensory vestiges of the past which we as viewers are offered. The music Julie hears is established as part of the *Concert pour l'Unification de l'Europe*, the unfinished work she will later complete with Olivier's aid (whether she herself has always written or contributed to her husband's music is left an open question). The lights she sees take material and visible form in the blue crystal mobile, the last object which remains in the blue room in the emptied house; these crystals later hang in Julie's apartment in the rue Mouffetard and become a focus of the more abstract play of colour and light within the film.

Where the music and blue light have a literal status in the narrative, their aesthetic function in the film and for the viewer might be considered further. Kieślowski's use of music, for example, is striking. The music we hear in *Bleu* is sometimes revealed to have its source within the scene: the flute played by the busker in the rue Mouffetard, the piano played by Olivier as he composes with Julie. Yet equally there are instances when the music appears to be entirely extradiegetic and to be used to augment the emotions and actions presented in the images of the film, to function artificially, but with certain semantic resonance (as we have seen in the contiguity between the words of the *Concert* we hear and the images of Julie's mother we see). In the most complex instance, however, the music of the film is shown to have its source materially, in Julie's mind, as in the instances when she is shown to hear music, to be startled by its sound, yet no source is evident. And here the question whether music in *Bleu* has a denotative or connotative function becomes particularly difficult. In other words, is the viewer given to believe that the sounds we hear are the sounds Julie hears in her mind (in a lyrical and abstract form of interior monologue), or does Kieślowski select music to connote and echo the state and tremors of Julie's psyche? It seems in effect that in *Bleu* the use of music is simultaneously mimetic and expressive, objective and subjective. Julie's mind becomes an echo chamber in which we hear the music of the film and through which we come to know its resonance.

The same argument might be put forward about the use of colour in *Bleu*, an issue which I have discussed at greater length elsewhere.[16] The blue lights of Julie's mental disturbance, and of her literal blue crystals, are linked visually with the ravishing swimming scenes which slip through the film. These again seem to suggest the polyvalency of Kieślowski's images. On a literal level Julie swims: the pool becomes a point of refuge in the film. This has been read as a return to the semiotic;[17] it has been seen also as a repeated sequence of drowning, resurrection and rebirth.[18] Yet Julie might be seen more to attempt to drown her memory than to drown herself. In visual terms, the viewer is presented with a shimmering spectacle of blue water and reflected blue light; the pool seems cavernous, enclosing. Julie's body is rendered an abstract shape as she swims. It seems that her mind becomes abstract too. As she emerges from the pool we experience the blankness of her mind and her sudden absence from herself. The pool exists literally, yet also becomes in visual and spatial terms the objective correlative of Julie's memory and of her state of mind. Within the film these swimming scenes afford moments of near abstraction, interludes of sensory pleasure and clear, almost turquoise blue light.

Kieślowski's film here seeks to maintain varying modes of representation: the viewer is called on to draw into question the relation between the literal and the figurative, the visual and the mental, the sensory and the hallucinatory. In some senses, and deliberately I think, the film does not cohere. It is fissured and shot through with scenes which come close to abstraction and undo the narrative teleology of the film, returning us time and again to the absence and unspoken trauma that is its point of departure. In this way, the moments of involuntary memory and traumatic disturbance are transposed and expressed in cinematic terms, yet not entirely resolved and embedded in the filmic narrative. In the representations of Julie's unwilled recall, the jolts in her survival, Kieślowski finds and constructs a cinematic analogue for the flashback of psychic trauma. In *Bleu*, Julie's memories and absences, their music and light, have no firm place in the past (these are not past events re-presented), nor in the present (where they represent interruption, not action). These images, in evoking the absence of the past and the disruption of the present, are not fully understood either by the protagonist or, it might be said, by the viewer.

Kieślowski thus achieves, in *Bleu*, a representation of memory disturbance and an evocation of the disintegrative effect of traumatic flashback. These moments of involuntary memory unsettle the viewer's experience and transform the surface texture of the film. Kieślowski thus works within and beyond the parameters of Deleuze's analysis in *Cinéma 2: L'Image-temps*. He explores the temporalization of the image and its disturbance. This is effected in the very denial of imaging and representation, as the mimetic reconstruction of mental pictures is abandoned, and the relation to the past, a constant concern in the film, necessarily remains a point of absence.

ix Survival

What remains for us to question finally is the ultimate issue of survival in *Bleu*. This reading will of necessity be ambivalent: I have suggested that *Bleu* is a film of survival in forgetting and denial, yet that denial itself leaves the protagonist, and viewer, prey to intrusive moments of involuntary memory which effectively render survival precarious. Is there a question of cure in Kieślowski's cinema of psychic disturbance? And what is the status of the ending of such a film?

Critics have, almost unquestioningly, found redemption at the end of *Bleu*. Claude-Marie Trémois and Vincent Remy, interviewing Kieślowski for *Télérama*, suggest: 'la fin de *Bleu* est optimiste, puisque Julie arrive à pleurer'.[19] Kieślowski replies: 'Vous trouvez? Pour moi, l'optimisme, ce serait plutôt des amants enlacés qui s'éloignent au soleil couchant. Ou au soleil levant, comme vous voulez. Mais si vous trouvez ça optimiste, pourquoi pas...'. The film seems to placate its optimistic viewers: the *Concert* is completed and its opulent music plays over the mental collage of the coda. The ending in unification and reparation seems perhaps one of the weakest and most artificial parts of the film. In this ending Kieślowski embodies the hopes of Olivier, Julie's lover, who has placed her in a position to finish the *Concert*. She is seen reflected in his eye and it is in his love that she is seen supposedly to survive and exist at the end of the film.

We see Julie in tears in the parting image: it may be that she has gained access to her grief and can latterly initiate the process of mourning which the film has shown cannot yet take place. Yet I would argue that if this is her survival, it comes at the expense of her memory, in the subsidence of her symptoms rather than the recall of her trauma. If we analyse *Bleu* in the light of *Hiroshima mon amour*, we might argue that survival comes not in the speaking of the past, but in the movement on from the past, in the drowning of the past and in displacement. In both films desire becomes a means to betray and extinguish memory. Julie's severance of links, her literal movement out of the spaces of her past, allows her contingent survival.

Bleu is by no means tranquil in its ending: Julie's emotions are unspoken, while Juliette Binoche's face remains here almost un-readable, absent, reflecting, just perceptibly, both pathos and relief. The ending of the film institutes distance between music and image, between integration and loss. In its ambivalence it gains its power to disturb. Julie's liberty here is felt most palpably in her emergence from the past, her emergence from her memory and her absolute auto-nomy. The soundtrack may insistently echo with 'l'amour', yet it is not the other, or his love, which guarantees Julie's survival. Rather she herself has found a way to negotiate her relation to the other (both Olivier and others) and to construct herself and her own identity. Kieślowski represents here a moment of existential freedom where Julie exists in the present, in herself.

Bleu may take ethical risks in privileging denial over cure, forgetting over conscious recall. Kieślowski does not overlook the trauma of amnesia itself and the disruptive and destabilizing effects of involun-tary recall. This we watch in the experiences of the women played by Riva and Binoche. Kieślowski's cinema of memory disturbance holds its own reminders of disorientation for the viewer as she is placed in a position necessarily to share Julie's loss of consciousness and loss of the past. Kieślowski's filmmaking itself depends more generally on the loss of links and the suppression of evidence, on the disruption of teleology, and on uncanny recall and recollection. This necessarily has a dissociative effect for the viewer whose memory is itself disturbed in viewing the film.

Hiroshima mon amour survives and is remembered in *Trois Couleurs: Bleu*; yet what we remember is precisely the pain of forgetting, the necessary betrayal of living in the present. Kieślowski's film lacks the urgent historical subject matter of *Hiroshima mon amour*; his screen is resolutely *intimiste*, as we have seen. Yet Kieślowski continues and deepens Resnais's and Deleuze's work on images and memory, making memories themselves absent in his images, and making the viewer too subject to his cinema in denial.

Notes to Chapter 2

1. Krzysztof Kieślowski and Krzysztof Piesiewicz, *Trois Couleurs* (Paris, 1997), I, 67, 68, 68.
2. Emma Wilson, 'Re-viewing desire: love and death in Hiroshima', *La Chouette* 26 (1995), 18–25.
3. Marguerite Duras, *Hiroshima mon amour* (Paris, 1971), 110, 124.
4. In his discussion of traumatic neuroses in 'Beyond the Pleasure Principle' Freud argues that a wound or injury inflicted at the same time as mental trauma works as a rule against the development of a traumatic neurosis. *Penguin Freud Library 11. On Metapsychology* (London, 1985), 269–338, 285. The truth of this observation apart, it is telling that in both *Hiroshima mon amour* and *Bleu*, physical trauma is sought, as it were, to assuage the raging of mental trauma.
5. Deleuze, *Cinéma 2*, 75, 76, 75, 76 n, 163, 154.
6. Kieślowski, *Trois Couleurs* I, 107, 68, 68, 68.
7. Strictly speaking in *Hiroshima mon amour* it is the Japanese lover who selects the trauma as the narrative of the Frenchwoman's identity. Indeed she asks him why he has chosen to know about this rather than the thousands of other events of her life. Interestingly Duras allows the lover three replies: 'C'est là, il me semble l'avoir compris que tu es si jeune... si jeune, que tu n'es encore à personne précisément. Cela me plaît', 'C'est là, il me semble l'avoir compris, que j'ai failli... te perdre... et que j'ai risqué ne jamais te connaître' and 'C'est là, il me semble l'avoir compris, que tu as dû commencer à être comme aujourd'hui tu es encore' (*Hiroshima mon amour*, 81). These speeches are shown to be three options in the screenplay. Where the Japanese man's curiosity is shown to be curiously overdetermined, it remains beyond doubt that the Frenchwoman has offered him access to this narrative of her past. While she consciously denies the necessity of this narrative of trauma to her current amorous relations, this narrative necessarily becomes the performance of her identity she chooses (or is compelled) to repeat.
8. Kieślowski, *Trois Couleurs* I, 69, 69, 69, 70, 69.
9. Although the majority of Kieślowski's work has been in film, he worked in television with his *Decalogue* project. In some senses, from this point on in his work, film and television and their differing yet comparable spectatorial practices are closely interconnected.
10. Geoffrey Macnab, '*Trois Couleurs: Bleu*', *Sight and Sound* 3/11 (Nov. 1993), 54–5, 55, 55, 55.
11. Deleuze, *Cinéma 2*, 51, 51, 52, 54–5, 55, 55, 55.
12. Cathy Caruth, *Trauma: Explorations in Memory* (Baltimore, 1995), 152, 152, 152.
13. Maureen Turim, *Flashbacks in Film: Memory and History* (London, 1989), 220, 220.
14. Caruth, *Trauma*, 153.
15. Duras, *Hiroshima mon amour*, 10.
16. Emma Wilson, '*Three Colours: Blue*: Kieślowski and the postmodern subject', *Screen* 39/4 (Winter 1998), 349–62.
17. Emma Robinson, 'Memory, nostalgia and the cinematic postmodern', unpublished paper read at the 1996 *Screen* Studies Conference.

18. Dave Kehr, 'To save the world: Kieślowski's Three Colours trilogy', *Film Comment* 30/6 (Nov.–Dec. 1994), 10–20, 15.

19. Krzysztof Kieślowski, 'Je doute, je doute toujours' (interview), *Télérama hors-série* (Sept. 1993), 90–6, 96, 96.

CHAPTER 3

❖

Voyeurism and Futurity
Trois Couleurs: Blanc

1 *Le Mépris*

In *Trois Couleurs: Blanc* a large-sized poster for Godard's *Le Mépris* (1963)
hangs over the set. It is seen by the viewer in a scene which establishes
the relations between spectatorship, visual beauty and sexual betrayal
upon which the film depends. Here Karol,[1] a Polish hairdresser who
has lost his life and love in a Parisian divorce hearing, emerges from a
metro station with his compatriot Mikołaj. Karol has narrated the tale
of his lost love to Mikołaj in an intimate scene on the metro platform.
The terms in which Karol speaks of his love belie the imbrication in
his mind of vision and desire. Karol attempts to reveal his visual fantasy
to Mikołaj and to embody it within cinematic images.

The first image we capture as he points out the love object is the
film poster, illuminated in this night-time Paris scene. The viewer sees
Bardot's cascading blonde hair and full breasts (itself an incongruous
image to market Godard's deconstructive film). The image of Bardot,
though fairly small within the frame, seemingly draws our attention
away from café awnings below and a lighted window to the right of
the poster. Mikołaj thinks Bardot is Karol's object of desire and
teasingly agrees that she is beautiful. His amusement is counterpointed
by Karol's almost pitiful sincerity as the camera pulls Karol's face into
focus as he encourages his friend (and the viewer) to look again. The
film cuts to a close-up of the poster, now taking up the whole frame,
and in such fine focus that we can read the names of Godard and
Bardot. From this point of reference, and initial misrecognition, the
camera pans slowly to the left to rest finally on the lighted window,
the proper object of our visual attention and the illuminated screen on
which we will see the enactment of Karol's desires.

The patterns of displacement are telling here. As in *Bleu*, we find a scene of misrecognition which complicates our understanding. That Mikołaj should mistake Bardot for Karol's love is by no means insignificant. In this poster, Bardot is in fact surprisingly reminiscent of Julie Delpy, the actress who plays Karol's estranged wife Dominique.[2] This the viewer will recognize since images of Dominique have already appeared in the film. In more complex terms, the correlation created here between cinema poster and lighted window draws attention to the relation the film maintains between cinematic spectatorship and desiring viewing. In *Blanc*, the drama of desire and betrayal is never separable from the visual dynamics of cinema as art form.

The reference to *Le Mépris* serves to indicate the self-conscious awareness of the cinematic which pervades in *Blanc*. That Kieślowski's point of reference should be a film of the *Nouvelle Vague* which, despite its relative conventionality in comparison with other works by Godard, critically takes filmmaking itself as subject, is significant within my general argument about Kieślowski's French cinema.[3] Indeed, all the more aptly, it seems telling that *Le Mépris* is itself an early example of a co-production (Franco-Italian) and one which takes questions of language, interpretation and translation overtly into account. In the voice-over credits sequence which opens *Le Mépris* we hear: 'Le cinéma, disait André Bazin, substitue à notre regard un monde qui s'accorde à nos désirs. *Le Mépris* est l'histoire de ce monde.'[4] Kieślowski's concern in referring to *Le Mépris* is with the memory and survival of a certain generation of filmmaking, and, as I shall argue more particularly here, with a certain ideal of cinematic femininity, fostered and critiqued by Godard. This nostalgia for a period of filmmaking, and its images of women, is nevertheless undercut, as is so much in Kieślowski's work, by a recognition of loss, of the vanity and artifice of cinematic ideals. Despite its seeming retrospection, *Blanc*, Kieślowski's ironic black comedy, is itself an essay in cinematic art which, I shall argue, counterpoints and correlates twin obsessions with voyeurism and futurity.

Before addressing these issues further, I want to pause, as does *Blanc* itself, over the poster for Godard's film and what it might imply.[5] The appearance of the poster, rather than any footage or stills from the film, seems apt. Godard's Bardot, as she appears in the poster, is a stellar icon of blonde, visible femininity. The marketing here is supposedly at odds with the film, or at least with the majority of its representation of Bardot as Camille (who has short dark hair for the major part of the film). On one level, *Le Mépris* works to demystify the myth of femininity the poster ironically still represents. The film comes ten years into Bardot's acting career after she has been both courted and vilified by the French press.[6] Godard takes the image of Bardot and takes it apart. He analyses her appeal, as her lover and a slowly moving camera simultaneously name, isolate and frame her body parts in the notorious, glowing opening shots.[7] Even in this opening scene (which bears comparison with the opening of *Hiroshima mon amour* as discussed in the previous chapter), Bardot's body is constructed in dialogue, in language, as much as in images. It is always already seen in a mirror,[8] created as a reflection and confected image. As Nicole Brenez suggests: 'Le personnage de Camille Javal se définit, fondamentalement, comme un spectacle esthétique.'[9]

One may privilege the deconstructive, self-questioning aspects of Godard's treatment of femininity, yet the very disjunction between the film and its marketing is nevertheless a sign of the ambivalence which I would maintain surrounds Godard's presentation of femininity. In the opening scene of Bardot naked, ostensibly used to pacify the film's producers and audience alike, the eroticism of the image still unsettles analysis: the viewer may disavow the fracture of the icon the film latterly represents.[10] Here note Laura Mulvey's warning that 'while Godard was capable of defetishizing the cinema and illuminating the fetishistic imbrication between woman as appearance and the dissembling nature of the late capitalist commodity, his iconography of the feminine on the screen was never freed from a fetishistic gloss'.[11] This dynamic between defetishization and disavowal will be indicative in discussion of the reflection of cinematic femininity in *Blanc*. We may wonder about the place of women in the emergent capitalist economy of Kieślowski's post-communist filmmaking. Where is this glossy blonde in the reflecting glass of Kieślowski's cinema?

II Short Films about Love

Images of women hold a special place and fascination in Kieślowski's cinema, although interestingly his films have not as yet engendered a specific feminist critique. In a late documentary, *Seven Women of Different Ages* (1978), Kieślowski superimposes images of seven different women dancers, from a small child to a mature ballet teacher. His approach is lyrical and almost abstract, using black and white photography and concentrating on a limited series of spaces, gestures and dances. His interest appears to be in the ways in which the female form can be framed and viewed. His late documentaries create a discourse as much about vision itself as about the object viewed. This is reflected particularly, for example, in the documentary *Station* (1980), where in representing Warsaw's Central Railway station Kieślowski appears most interested in the images produced by the 'overhead video "spy" cameras'[12] which watch over the station. It seems telling that these two documentaries coincide with the period in which Kieślowski begins making feature films. It might be said that in his interest in vision, he becomes increasingly aware of the question of who is looking and why. Film as fictional narrative affords the possibility of constructing an overtly subjective vision, of exploring the ways in which any view of the world is necessarily partial and filtered. This growing emphasis, in Kieślowski's cinema, marks a move from an interest in the world viewed to an interest, in particular, in voyeurism.

Kieślowski's analysis of voyeurism is most protracted in *A Short Film about Love* (1989), the sixth film of *Decalogue*, which was also released in a longer version for the cinema. In the Warsaw housing estate which is the social and geographical space of *Decalogue*, a young postal worker, Tomek, becomes obsessed with his female neighbour, Magda, who lives in the apartment opposite. With his telescope trained on her window he watches her ritualistically undressing in her illuminated room. Kieślowski's interest in voyeurism here has inspired critics to make comparisons with *Rear Window* (1954), emphasizing in effect the Western influence which could be seen to be becoming more marked in Kieślowski's last Polish Films. Bernard Bénoliel hazards a fairly convincing interpretation of *A Short Film about Love* as a form of allegory about relations between East and West in Europe, arguing: 'le jeune Tomek, matant de sa fenêtre la belle Magda, répétait en privé le regard amoureux des démocraties populaires pour l'image inaccessible d'un Occident de rêve'.[13] Such a reading works well to propose implicit links between *A Short Film about Love* and *Blanc* which latterly appears to focus further on the ways in which East views West in Europe and how, after the fall of communism, the idealized image of the West is incorporated and consumed, in melancholy fashion, in the creation of a new economy and society.

I want to retain some caution, however, over the exclusive association between visual display, voyeurism and Western European culture. While this may be a dominant reading of late capitalism, I am reluctant, again, to suggest a specific demarcation between East and West in Kieślowski's filmmaking. The voyeurism which is his subject in *A Short Film about Love* and *Blanc* may link his filmmaking to Hollywood cinema which has treated visual pleasures so extensively and been itself the subject of analysis in such terms in feminist and psychoanalytic theory. Yet a film such as the documentary *Station* serves to remind Kieślowski's viewers again, I think, that vision and voyeurism may equally be associated with surveillance and with the specific visual monitoring of the society of which Kieślowski was himself first a product.[14]

In perpetuating a continuum between his Polish and French filmmaking, Kieślowski further associates and repeats the visual ideal of the voyeurist's desire. The enigmatic blonde woman is as much an ideal of his Polish filmmaking (and culture) as it is of his move to the West and filming of Delpy. In *A Short Film about Love* Magda is played by the Polish actress Grażyna Szapołowska who starred previously in *No End*. Kieślowski comments: 'when I looked through all the screen tests which we'd shot, at all the actresses available in Poland at that time, I realized that Szapołowska would be the best'.[15]

In many senses *A Short Film about Love* may be seen to prefigure the voyeurism which is the subject of *Blanc*: considered together the two films represent an on-going meditation on spectatorship and gender. What is most noticeable in *A Short Film about Love* is the way in which the power relations which subtend voyeurism are re-thought. This is particularly evident in the feature-length version of the film which contains a coda (absent in the television film) presenting a corrective to any fixed view of gender and viewing relations. Discussion of this coda will here be used to anticipate a more sustained discussion of voyeurism in *Blanc*.

In *A Short Film about Love*, Tomek falls in love with Magda and gradually manages to insinuate himself into her life. Eventually, in a crucial scene, she invites him into her apartment. Tomek appears in the room he has always watched with his telescope; he is now a protagonist on the screen the lighted window of Magda's apartment has become for him. But his performance fails all too literally: he tries to make love to her but comes too soon, failing to enter her.[16] He flees and in his humiliation commits suicide by cutting his wrists.[17] In the coda to the film, seemingly regretting Tomek's death, Magda makes a melancholy identification with him. She now enters his apartment, sits at his window and looks through his telescope. The film closes with an image of a female character as both viewer and voyeur, establishing a symmetry in its images of a face behind a telescope. But this alone is not the limit of Kieślowski's discourse on voyeurism, both erotic and cinematic.

Most importantly, the coda gives Magda and the viewer access to images which would otherwise have remained hidden or obscure for her. The coda entirely endorses a comparison between the act of viewing through a telescope and the act of viewing images in the cinema. Kieślowski uses a series of five close-ups of Magda's face as she looks through the telescope: her face is illuminated by under-lighting, giving the illusion that it is bathed in the reflected light of a movie screen. The film cuts between images of Magda viewing, and images of what she sees. As she first looks through the telescope the screen is blank, both for her and for the viewer. Then a door opens and we see Magda herself silhouetted, outlined in light as she enters her apartment. She switches on the light, and the performance, as it were, commences. The telescope gives Magda access to viewing herself, at a distance. She becomes the spectator viewing the screen created by the lighted window of her own apartment. The images viewed are shown only just perceptibly in slow motion, marking them out from the images of the film's main part. These images become essentially a film that Magda views: this is emphasized in the close-up images of her facial expression and her reactions.

The film Magda views is at first familiar to us as it appears made up of images we have seen previously from Tomek's perspective. As their internal narrative unfolds, however, it is clear that what we see now are impossible, recuperative images. Magda closes her eyes several times in the coda. As she looks at first her left eye is closed, her right eye narrowed so she can view through the telescope. The film appears to represent the literal act of vision, even if the images viewed are imaginary. The images at first appear to be a projection into the future as Magda allows herself to pre-view what will happen after she returns to her own apartment. In the third close-up of her face, however, both her eyes are shown to be closed. She cannot look through the telescope, yet the film cuts again to the image of the lighted window. Here the viewer sees an act of imaginary resurrection and apparent wish-fulfilment. If Magda's eyes are closed we must now, we assume, have access to the images she sees in her mind's eye as she fantasizes Tomek's return, his presence in her apartment, and her own gesture of tenderness as she reaches up to stroke his face.

In this coda, and its displaced act of voyeurism, Kieślowski works to call into question the relation between the virtual and the actual we have seen haunting his cinema throughout this study. *A Short Film about Love* might be seen to suggest indeed that the voyeur's prime object viewed is essentially only ever the product of his (and her?) own fantasy. Kieślowski draws voyeurism into question, making us think further, in particular about power, fantasy and wish-fulfilment. These are the issues which I will look at further in *Blanc*, in dialogue with feminist film theory.

III Voyeurism

Film theory has depended on a fairly fixed model of spectatorship, which carries with it a specific view of voyeurism: this is displayed optimally in the work of Christian Metz. As Carol Clover sums things up: 'for Metz [...] the viewer necessarily identifies with the camera in an operation that is essentially assaultive'.[18] She continues: 'Metz argues that because cinema is predicated on a distance between the spectator and the object of vision [...] the cinematic spectator is necessarily a voyeur, and voyeurism, with its drive to mastery, is by nature sadistic.' Clover herself is one of those feminist film theorists who have sought to re-think spectatorship, and in particular the fixed relation established between voyeurism, sadism and mastery. Her work, like that of Linda Williams and others, has been important in thinking through possible masochistic pleasures in spectatorship, and in opening up a whole repertoire of identificatory positions for the film spectator. Williams in particular has identified the limits of gaze theory itself, and of the counter-arguments of its first generation of feminist critics. She argues that 'any theory of spectatorship must now be historically specific, grounded in the specific spectatorial practices, the specific narratives, *and* the specific attractions of a mobilized and embodied gaze of viewers. There are a great many viewing positions, a great many "ways of seeing" in classical, modernist and post-modernist spectatorship.'[19]

This call for a mobilized, finely inflected theory of spectatorship seems of importance in affording a more developed understanding of the complexities of the reception of film. My interest here is in the specific case of films which consciously take spectatorship as subject and reflect back to the spectator a view of themselves viewing. *Blanc* is a case in point. Film theorists have consistently looked elsewhere, at different genres and at avant-garde filmmaking, in order to image or imagine different spectatorial practices. Mulvey looked towards the work of 'radical filmmakers'.[20] Carol Clover has worked on horror and spectatorship in *Men, Women and Chainsaws*; Williams has worked on pornography in *Hard Core*. While not denying the importance of genre to our re-thinking of spectatorship, I want to inquire whether, in looking in the same places, in narrative cinema, we can already find different images.

In both *A Short Film about Love* and *Blanc* Kieślowski appears to take as his subject the fixed viewing relations we find placed in cinematic narrative from *Panique* (1946) or *Rear Window* (1954) through *Atlantic City USA* (1980) and *Monsieur Hire* (1988) to such post-modern travesties as *Sliver* (1991) or *Addicted to Love* (1997). In my view, Kieślowski constructs this apparatus in order effectively to dismantle it. Here (following Williams) I would say that a historical as well as national and political understanding of his filmmaking is useful. Following the discussion of *La Double Vie de Véronique* above, it might be said that Kieślowski creates a retrospective homage to one of the recurring obsessions of narrative cinema. And it is in this perspective that the poster from *Le Mépris* fills the frame of his film. Kieślowski returns to the locus of voyeurism, indeed, in order to see it differently. That different perspective comes in part from his emergence in a different tradition and culture (although, as I have argued, voyeurism is itself always also present within Kieślowski's Polish filmmaking and the society he analyses). Further, his perspective is inflected temporally given his status as latecomer in the field of representation of voyeurism and other cinematic perversions. Kieślowski's cinematic contribution to an on-going visual and theoretical debate is to explore and elucidate the confusion between virtual and actual in voyeurism, and the ways in which this unsettles the supposed mastery of the voyeur. In order to show how he does this I will go back through Metz to re-think relations between voyeurism and mastery.

Blanc is, as we have seen, the visual narrative of a Polish hairdresser, Karol Karol, who has married a French model, Dominique. It is a bilingual film, set part in Paris, part in Warsaw, which takes as one of its ostensible subjects difficulties in translation between East and West in Europe, between Polish and French and between male and female.[21] Kieślowski might be seen here, as in *La Double Vie de Véronique*, to dramatize again the very constraints of his work as Polish *auteur* in the French film industry. Yet in the revolutionary schema of the trilogy, *Blanc* represents Equality, and attempts again to establish parity between East and West in Europe and a lack of difference between the style of filmmaking in East and West.[22] Equality also has its own implications for viewing relations in the film. *Blanc* is a film about equality between the sexes, in power and in vision, in ways which challenge some of the dominant tenets of feminist film theory.

As I have been arguing, voyeurism is the key to *Blanc*. The film all but opens with the literal separation between Karol and Dominique in a court of law. Their divorce renders legal the distance between them, which itself affords Karol his position as voyeur. As Metz has argued, following Freud, voyeurism always keeps apart the object and the source of the drive, here the eye. Metz writes: 'the voyeur is very careful to maintain a gulf, an empty space, between the object and the eye, the object and his own body'.[23] He continues: 'The voyeur represents in space the fracture which forever separates him from the object; he represents his very dissatisfaction.' *Blanc* makes Karol's dissatisfaction its subject in both spatial and psychological terms. Dominique becomes the necessary object of his voyeuristic fantasy and of his literal voyeurism. This is suggested specifically in the visual style or stylization of a series of shots of Julie Delpy which run through the film, and which establish her as glossy object of desire. Before looking at these further, and in order to understand their significance more fully, it will be useful to consider some questions of temporality in *Blanc*.

IV Flashforward

Blanc is distinguished in Kieślowski's filmmaking by its overt use of the flashforward. From the start Kieślowski renders our apprehension of the teleology of the film uncertain. The film opens, like the other films in the trilogy, with a mechanical moving image, here a trunk moving along a luggage conveyor belt. After the titles sequence, shots of this trunk thus mechanically conveyed are intercut with the opening scenes of the narrative. At this juncture shots of the trunk hold no overt sense for the first-time viewer, and seemingly no relation to the film's protagonist Karol, whom we watch arriving at the Palais de Justice,[24] then divorced from his resplendent wife, and abandoned in Paris. The shots of the trunk punctuate the first scene, but we are left only to wonder about their meaning and temporal status. This becomes clearer as we encounter the shots again, now in their correct place in the narrative sequence. Karol, divorced and destitute in Paris, meets Mikołaj, a fellow Pole, as he plays a Polish tune on a comb in the metro. As Karol has no passport Mikołaj transports him back to Poland in a trunk. It is this clandestine transportation we witness obliquely in the first shots. The sense and place of the shots in the narrative can only be understood retrospectively, but even then questions remain for the viewer.

On one level it appears simply that Kieślowski eschews neatly chronological narrative, allowing flashforwards to disrupt the viewer's apprehension of the sequence of the film, and to stress that the narrative is artificially constructed through montage and can best be understood in non-linear terms. On a further level, as viewers, we may begin to question also notions of cause and effect, through this disruption of chronological sequence. The anterior presence, and later recurrence, of the shots of the trunk seem to suggest that the film seeks to disclose the stages which lead to Karol's enclosure in the mock coffin his trunk resembles. Further still, we may begin to perceive that the flashforwards serve also to represent the protagonist's state of mind, his precipitation and mental buffeting, intercut visibly with the visual narrative of his physical circumstances. The flashforward serves then to place the relation between the virtual and the actual in the image in question.

These comments, and my reading of the trunk scene, may be productively compared with Deleuze's work on the time-image. Deleuze does not raise the specific issue of the flashforward (neither does Turim more than fleetingly). This notion of the flashforward indeed might be seen to be paradoxical for Deleuze given his theorization of virtuality and the time-image which depends on an event and the simultaneous and later retrospective recording of a layer of memories or traces of that event. There seems to be no space here for the anticipation of such an event in a virtual image.[25] In debating this question through Kieślowski, I want to look at Deleuze's work on the flashback and at how this concept is itself re-worked by Kieślowski in his manipulation of the flashforward.

Deleuze discusses the flashback in his work on the time-image. As we have seen in previous chapters, Deleuze reveals that in the mechanism of the flashback and related visual and structuring devices, film can draw attention precisely to the relation between the real and the imaginary, the physical and the mental, the objective and the subjective, and specifically the virtual and the actual. The flashback, and its use in cinematic narrative, has a specific bearing on our understanding of the representation of destiny and necessity in films. He argues that the flashback constructs an illusion of determinism and causality, offering as it does a supposedly explanatory response to the questions of cause and effect raised in a specific cinematic narrative. Here we might ask whether the same can be said of the flashforward and the image which anticipates the future rather than re-presents the past.

The future is, of course, at least anticipated in Deleuze's work on memory in the cinema. He argues: 'C'est dans le présent qu'on se fait une mémoire, pour s'en servir dans le futur quand le présent sera passé.'[26] Memory is directed towards the future, though created in the present. While Deleuze, following Bergson, describes a mental process and its temporalities, his thoughts here have a peculiar resonance for cinema as medium which embodies its own temporality in its very apparatus. In describing the cinematic signifier, in his work on voyeurism, Metz reminds us of the temporal *décalage* upon which cinema depends, where the time of shooting and the time of projection and viewing do not coincide.[27] In these terms cinema itself is a commemorative art in its specificity, and is potentially self-reflexive implicitly or explicitly when it takes memory as its subject. So, for Deleuze, the recording and representation of memory both in films and for the viewer potentially anticipates a future position when the current present will be past. For Kieślowski, film can itself seek to anticipate and pre-present this future position: it is in these terms that Kieślowski re-configures the time-image as theorized by Deleuze.

The flashforward as used by Kieślowski, like the flashback as described by Deleuze, draws our attention to relations between virtual and actual images, but, in a different way from the flashback, the flashforward causes us to re-think questions of causality. In Kieślowski's cinema indeed, causality itself, so readily associable with questions of time and destiny, will also be seen to intertwine, more arrestingly, with questions of spectatorship and subjective vision.

v Causality

In addition to the shots of the trunk, several further flashforwards thread through the course of *Blanc*. These take the form of Dominique entering a room seen partly in silhouette.[28] They are by no means as easily perceptible for the viewer as the shots of the trunk. Dave Kehr comments specifically on these flashforwards: 'Kieślowski uses quick, enigmatic flashforwards (such as the shots of Dominique entering an unknown hotel room in *White*) to give a fatefulness to the proceedings. Whether or not we consciously register these images (and many people do not), they create a feeling of resonance and fulfilment when they recur in the course of the narrative (it's the room Dominique checks into when Karol succeeds in luring her back to Warsaw).'[29] For Kehr these flashforwards serve primarily to anticipate and pre-view their own proper place in the film. His understanding of them, on one level, is purely structural and such a reading serves to emphasize the fact that Kieślowski's films are composite pieces which depend on a complex notion of montage and at times atemporal ordering. Kehr's only concern with psychology relates specifically to the psychology of spectatorship. He suggests, as we have seen, that these flashforwards, perceived consciously or not, make a particular impression on the viewer and lend, he says specifically, a sense of fatefulness to the viewer's understanding of the film's exegesis. My conclusions about these flashforwards are more ambivalent.

Kehr interprets the flashforwards, I assume, as actual images which belong to a different time scale from that of the place in the narrative where they are inserted: in this sense they might be compared to the shots of the trunk. Yet in my analysis of these shots of the trunk above I attempted to show that they serve to reveal a psychical reality, whilst also literally anticipating future action. This is even more the case, and more self-consciously, in the second example of the flashforwards of Dominique. Here Kieślowski gives his viewers access, if briefly, to the image patterns of Karol's imagination, to his inner cinema. The first flashforward of Dominique comes after Karol's return to Poland and after his emergence from the despair and lethargy which mark his first days there. He stands on a riverbank, about to throw in a two-franc piece, the only coin he has brought from Paris. The camera closes in on his face and we see it suddenly receptive, suddenly lit up with an idea to which the film then cuts: there follows the supposed flashforward of Dominique entering the hotel bedroom. The scene functions to reveal the motivation behind Karol's ambition as he will work himself up to a position of financial power in the second part of the film (as Kieślowski offers us a trenchant, yet typically disengaged account of the economy and mechanisms of post-communist Poland). The film reveals how Karol constructs an imaginary scenario: the return of his wife, her re-entry into the space of his desire. The opening of the space of this fantasy in Karol's mind is reflected both in the way the scene is presented visually and in its specific subject. In the blankness of the screen, and the blankness of Karol's mind, a door is seen to open and Dominique is seen to enter.

This scene exists primarily as a virtual image and as a revelation of the spaces of Karol's imagination. Yet what remains uncanny in the film is that it also holds the more literal status of a flashforward since, as Kehr has remarked, the scene which, following my argument, Karol imagines, is finally inserted into the narrative sequence of the film. What we see as viewers is the fact that Karol has managed to choreograph his fantasy down to the last detail so that the scene we view in its proper chronological sequence perfectly repeats the virtual scenario Karol has viewed in his imagination. *Blanc* reveals how identical shots, shown in a different place in a filmic narrative, can hold different meanings. Kieślowski's achievement is to reveal how a memory trace can be created not only after the event, or indeed at the moment of an event as Deleuze has pointed out, but even uncannily before that event has happened. Karol is offered, in the space of the film, the opportunity to live out his inner fantasy, to disturb the divide between psychical and material reality in Freud's terms, as Kieślowski as filmmaker denies the division, in Deleuze's terms, between virtual and actual images in the cinema. In this sense Kieślowski shows his protagonist seeking a directive control over his destiny.

This search for control relates directly to the question of destiny in representation and the apprehension of fate by the spectator. For Deleuze, the flashback offers an illusion of causality; for Kehr, the flashforward creates an impression of fatefulness for the viewer. Central to my argument about *Blanc* in particular, and Kieślowski's cinema more generally, is an anxiety about such supposed determinism and its relation to any realist representation of fate, destiny and human motivation. These issues can be usefully debated through Žižek's work in *Looking Awry*. Žižek explores the way in which we apprehend the ending of a film as something that naturally and organically follows from the preceding action; he argues that if the ending were to be changed this too would be experienced by viewers as something that developed naturally out of earlier events. He concludes that this is possible precisely because 'the experience of a linear "organic" flow of events is an illusion (albeit a necessary one) that masks the fact that it is the ending that *retroactively* confers the consistency of an organic whole on the preceding events'.[30] It is in these terms that cinema offers such a distracting illusion of direction and destiny. As Žižek points out: 'What is masked is the radical contingency of the enchainment of narration, the fact that, at every point, things might have turned out otherwise.' He suggests that this radical contingency can be made visible by proceeding in a reverse way, by presenting the events backwards, from the end to the beginning. He offers several examples of works which adopt such a retrospective structure, and suggests that 'such reversals in the order of narration might be expected to provoke an effect of total fatalism: everything is decided in advance, while the protagonists, like puppets, unwittingly play out their roles in an already written script'. Yet in fact, as he argues, 'it is precisely the reversal of the temporal order that makes us experience in an almost palpable way the utter contingency of the narrative sequence, i.e., the fact that, at every turning point, things might have taken another direction'.

The question of how things might have been, and of the radical plurality of fate, particularly obsesses Kieślowski. He has ac-knowledged: 'I believe fate is an important part of life. Of all our lives, my own included. [...] Naturally, a person may select his or her own path through life and so to a certain extent determines what happens along the way. But to understand where you are in the present, it is necessary to retrace the steps of your life and isolate the parts played by necessity, free will and pure chance.'[31] Kieślowski appears to use cinema as a means to engage with these questions: this can be felt palpably, as we have seen, in *Blind Chance* which offers three separate visual narratives, revealing three different existential paths the protagonist's life might take. It is only retrospectively that the viewer may perceive the absurdly determining role that a single moment may have in the protagonist's destiny; and it is only from her artificially omniscient standpoint that the viewer can perceive the parallel destinies to which any individual, to retain some semblance of sanity, must remain blind.

For Žižek, narrative consistency, and by implication existential destiny, are retroactive illusions. Arguably he nevertheless ac-knowledges their necessity.[32] For Kieślowski, cinema itself has been a means to disclose this retroactive illusion of consistency, by showing divergent narrative and existential paths in *Blind Chance* for example, or by refusing any recourse to explanatory flashback in *Bleu*. In *Blanc*, he takes his experimentation with the imbrication of the cinematic and the psychological one stage further.

Kieślowski's use of the flashforward draws causality into question:

in the double status of the images we view, Kieślowski on the one hand allows us the pleasure of recognition and determinism, of pre-views of the future, yet on the other reveals this determinism to be an illusion consciously constructed in this instance by the protagonist, and more generally, in cinema, by the filmmaker who deliberately controls the enchainment of the narrative.

Karol is seen to refuse the very contingencies of destiny in a search to control and choreograph his own life. The viewer may experience a sense of recognition and concomitant fatefulness in the flashforwards of the film. This is because Karol has himself chosen to adopt the position of cinematic viewer of his own life: he seeks to enact the dramas of his imagination, to offer himself the illusory position of mastery of the cinema spectator who views images from a distance. This is compounded in the film in the visual similarity—soft-focus golden light and silhouetted figure—between the scene where Dominique enters the space of his fantasy which Karol obsessively stages in his imagination, and scenes where Karol, as voyeur, literally watches Dominique from a distance. It is at this juncture that we return to the question of voyeurism that is central to this chapter.

vi Dominique

The recurrence of shots of Julie Delpy as Dominique, blonde, polished, impervious, operates as a central mechanism in *Blanc*. These images are marked by a golden, part-filtered light, pronounced shadows and the image of Delpy in silhouette. She is first seen like this in the hairdressing salon she and Karol have owned together. In this originary image we will see an actual shot of Dominique and Karol together which becomes in effect a source of virtual fantasy. This scene of filtered light, where the faithless object of desire is viewed projected, a moving and tactile shadow against a vertical blind, is the space of Karol's fantasy. Dominique's image is de-realized here in a scene which appears proto-cinematic in its visual emphasis on the projection of shadow images and the space of the blind as screen. Equally this image recalled would seem to take the form of a screen memory for Karol, a memory in whose boundaries he may deny his loss of Dominique. This image is recalled as Karol watches Dominique's lighted window from below in the street in Paris and sees her shadow now falling on the curtains as she makes love with another man.[33] It is recalled again in the two supposed flashforwards which briefly interrupt the temporal course of the film as Dominique's figure is seen in silhouette against a lighted doorframe, and further in the scene these flashforwards anticipate (temporally and psychologically) where Dominique, silhouetted, enters her hotel bedroom to find her supposedly dead husband naked in her bed. Finally Dominique is fixed behind a window frame, in prison, in the closing scene of the film.

Despite their differing status (between virtual and actual) these scenes are distinguished and correlated visually. In addition they afford a specific set of viewing relations, functioning effectively to reflect (on) the very act of viewing in the cinema. Linking these scenes is a spectatorship relation which is essentially voyeuristic. For Metz, voyeurism in the cinema differs from that of other scopic regimes. He argues: 'The cinema is profoundly different from the theatre as also from more intimate voyeuristic activities with a specifically erotic aim [...]: cases where voyeurism remains linked to exhibitionism, where the two faces, active and passive, of the component drive are by no means dissociated.'[34] In this sense, the voyeurism figured in *Blanc* might be distinguished from cinematic voyeurism *per se*, in Metz's terms, since the relation between voyeur and exhibitionist appears most properly Kieślowski's subject. This we witness directly in *A Short Film about Love* where Magda is seen disquietingly to perform for Tomek as he watches, verifying that he is there by phoning him. In *Blanc* Dominique is viewed unawares as she makes love, silhouetted in the lighted window. But Karol then telephones her, attempting in a sense to make himself present in the scene from which he is separated. Dominique performs her pleasure for him, letting him hear her come over the phone. Here Kieślowski exploits the invocatory drive as well as the scopic drive: Metz maintains the equivalent dependence on distance of the two drives, although he comments that the invocatory has been less closely studied than the scopic. Kieślowski himself repeatedly makes the invocatory drive his subject, as in the recorded sound patterns of *La Double Vie de Véronique* or the Judge's voyeuristic activities, listening in on the conversations of his neighbours in *Rouge*.

In *Blanc*, then, in both visual and aural terms, the distance between voyeur and object of desire is maintained, but the fixity of the power relations enacted is by no means as certain. Karol has stated in the court where his divorce is made legal that he needs time to save his marriage; he says (in Polish): 'Je ne crois pas qu'il n'y ait plus de sentiments entre nous.'[35] It is this bind and condition that is tested as the film unfolds. For Dominique, the performance of her desire appears exacerbated by the presence of her lovesick husband. Karol not only desires her, but is a witness to her desirability, and a victim of her passion. Her exhibitionism is seen to be startlingly complicit with Karol's voyeurism; but it is her exhibitionism which is figured here as sadistic, as motivated ironically by a drive to mastery. For Karol, the lighted window of voyeuristic desire becomes the locus of loss and betrayal. His position is seen to be masochistic, and this is tangibly emphasized in the first episodes as we see him frequently bruised and knocked about. In the first place, then, Kieślowski's cinema appears literally and simply to invert the terms of sadism and masochism, activity and passivity of the relation between voyeur and exhibitionist. But this is by no means all that *Blanc* achieves in its imbrication of voyeurism and futurity.

Dominique's performance in the lighted window is, as I have argued, the locus of Karol's fantasy. In the visual markers Kieślowski chooses, he creates a direct equivalence between the actual images of Dominique that Karol has viewed and the virtual images of her that he constructs in his imagination (comparisons with Resnais's *L'Année dernière à Marienbad* (1961) seem called for here). Karol's external position as masochistic voyeur is internalized as he re-views his illuminated images of Dominique in the inner cinema of his imagination. As spectators, we ourselves are placed in a position to share Karol's mental images. The latter half of the film, relocated in Warsaw, concerns Karol's rise to a position of financial power in the nascent economy of post-communist Poland. His actions are motivated here, in every sense, by his relation to Dominique and his separation from her. This is demonstrated literally to the spectator as the flashforwards or mental images of Dominique are intercut with the narrative of Karol's rise to financial power. Dominique's image motivates Karol's ambition.[36] He acts to allow her to become, in time, his witness, his viewer, as well as his object of desire.

In the last scene of the film Dominique's figure is seen again at a lighted window. She has been imprisoned, literally, as she is caught metaphorically in the voyeur/exhibitionist relations upon which Karol's desire has depended. The roles of the couple have swapped significantly: Karol appears to have assumed the sadistic dimensions of his role as voyeur, and Dominique, now in prison in Poland, is the victim of his desire. Is this an affirmation of the fixed viewing relations I have been arguing Kieślowski may be seen to critique? Or is this itself an affirmation of equality, of the equal but opposite relations upon which desire, in this exaggerated form of role play, might be seen to depend? I would argue that *Blanc* explores the possibility of a shift in power relations, of an unsettling of the supremacy of the male desiring subject. Here, specifically, the notion of performance is significant: Dominique at the lighted window again performs for Karol, but here she mimes herself putting a wedding ring on her finger, recognizing the bind which makes her complicit in relations with Karol, the bind which Karol has named, for better or worse, a bind of love. Equality and complicity are established between Karol and Dominique as he weeps watching her illuminated image, as she has wept, viewed in sudden close-up through opera glasses, as Karol watches his own funeral.

If *Blanc* does indeed establish equality and interchange in the viewing relations it takes as its subject, does this in itself have any impact on our understanding of cinematic spectatorship as a form of voyeurism? As I suggested earlier, Metz distinguishes between cinematic voyeurism and that of other scopic regimes. He draws on the specificity of the cinematic signifier, as he defines it. The cinematic signifier depends on the literal absence of the object seen, creating a temporal and spatial distance (as we saw in discussion above of cinema as a commemorative art form). Metz argues: 'in the cinema, the actor was present when the spectator was not (=shooting), and the spectator is present when the actor is no longer (=projection): a failure to meet of the voyeur and exhibitionist whose approaches no longer coincide (they have "missed" one another).'[37] Here the spectator is placed in a position of solitude and solipsism: cinematic spectatorship depends, for Metz, on this failure, and further on a recognition of the status of the cinematic signifier and illusion. He states, indeed: 'It is understood that the audience is not duped by the diegetic illusion, it "knows" that the screen presents no more than a fiction.' What Metz fails to explore here is the specific status of the cinematic fiction which mirrors and re-presents the spectator's own activity, making voyeurism itself its subject. It is in these terms that Kieślowski's cinema allows or compels its spectator to recognize the drama of viewing in which she is necessarily engaged. And in so doing, Kieślowski presents us with a drama which denies the failure and solitude upon which cinematic voyeurism has been seen to be based.

For Kieślowski, the act of viewing, as represented in *Blanc*, depends entirely on uncanny recognition. Whenever Julie switches on the television in *Bleu* she finds her own life represented back to her; the Judge in *Rouge* witnesses the survival of Valentine through the medium of the televisual screen; even Véronique watches a marionette show which uncannily represents her own life. Kieślowski's protagonists find a performance of their identities and life histories projected for them as they adopt a spectatorial position. This is illustrated most clearly in the coda to *A Short Film about Love*. By making viewing itself his subject Kieślowski allows the screen to become a mirror where, at least in part, the viewer perceives the performance and even the satisfaction of her desires. His films work in temporal terms to anticipate their own viewing. Spectatorship itself is a matter of futurity. Kieślowski seeks to foster an illusion of complicity between viewer and representation. His films demonstrate knowledge of the viewer's future presence in their anterior reflection of spectatorship. Thus his films may be seen to deconstruct or disavow the division drawn by Metz between cinematic and other forms of voyeurism.

Kieślowski's films work to unsettle the norms of voyeurism both represented and enacted in the cinema. The difference between active and passive, between sadist and masochist, is not denied or solely inverted, but deconstructed where spectatorial positions are effectively mobilized (Williams's terms) and unfixed. The status of the image itself is equally placed in question: the images in the lighted frame figure at once deliberate performance and projected fantasy, as the division between virtual and actual is denied. Our confidence as viewers is unsettled by the very uncertainty of the images and spectatorial positions afforded us. A series of internal reflections deepens and deflects Kieślowski's cinematic representations, yet as viewers we may yet glimpse our own image reflected there. Kieślowski's cinema represents voyeurism to its viewer, yet its final achievement is to allow us no mastery over the images viewed.

VII 'Un mariage blanc'

Blanc creates uncertainty in the mind of its viewer in one further, significant, set of subjective images. Here doubt arises as to whose inner vision we share: Kieślowski seeks to envisage here an example of inner intersubjectivity. Where equality has been his theme in *Blanc*, and exchange of viewing positions a structural device in *A Short Film about Love*, as well as in *Blanc* itself, here Kieślowski tests further the possibility of equivalence between viewing positions, and equivalent investment in an individual memory. That this memory should commemorate the union of the two individuals concerned is itself significant.

True to the colour of its title, *Blanc* is haunted by a spectral image of a white wedding (or *mariage en blanc*). This image appears first intersecting the scene of Karol's divorce. The judge asks him whether his marriage was consummated. The film cuts from Karol's figure to a flashback to his wedding day. The flashback takes the form of a forwards tracking shot, offering Karol's perspective as he leaves the church with Dominique by his side. The light is filtered and softened, the ephemeral gauze of Dominique's veil catching its reflections. The sounds of the courtroom are superimposed over the flashback. Although we hear Dominique's heels as she walks back down the aisle, we also hear Karol's negative response to the judge's interrogation. No, his marriage was not consummated. As Dominique and Karol emerge from the church, photographers rush to take their picture, and the pigeons which have settled on the church's façade rise up, the sound of their wings echoing here as elsewhere in the film. An image, out of focus, of the white flowers on Dominique's veil almost blocks our view, until she turns and is seen, completely beautiful in close-up, smiling, her hands raised to her face and almost translucent.

Each detail, the perspective and the very gloss of the image, persuade the viewer that she is party specifically to Karol's idealized image of marriage. Yet the film cuts from the flashback immediately to another image of Delpy's face in close-up, now imaged as she stands to bear witness in the divorce court. Does the film cut merely from Karol's past memory of Dominique to his present witnessing of her? Or does she share this memory with Karol? Is the flashback hers as much as his? Evidence later in the film seems to point further to intersubjectivity as a prime concern of these memory sequences.

The second flashback to the marriage comes as Dominique is arrested in Poland. She sits for a moment, her face lit up in half profile and then the familiar sound of pigeons infiltrates the scene and the film cuts to the aisle once more. The memory or fantasy is interrupted on this viewing before the couple emerges from the church and the film cuts now to an image of Karol in contemplation as he combs his hair. The sound of Dominique's heels echoes still, seemingly an aural reminder of the memory trace which plays in Karol's mind as we now view his face absorbed. He looks through his comb as if he could picture a virtual image of his marriage through this filter. The film cuts then once more from his face to the couple's emergence from the church. The sequence of shots appears to be repeating those we have seen earlier on in the film. Yet, viewed closely, differences can be observed. Dominique now does not stop and smile, almost overwhelmed, but turns to kiss Karol. As we see their mouths touching, his eyes are closed, while hers open briefly to observe his face. Now their two faces are in close-up, and their pale skin fills the frame as the image fades to white and a blank screen.

While the major perspective of the film is Karol's, the film's editing and the unsolicited view of Dominique's eyes open, work to make us wonder whether she shares Karol's memories too and returns as obsessively to their visual traces. Such nostalgia might indeed be the motivation for her mime in the film's closing frames where, as we have seen, caught in prison Dominique demonstrates her desire to marry Karol once more and effectively to re-stage the memory we have viewed in flashback. But remember the non-coincidence of the two flashback sequences. That there are differences between the two memorial replays of the wedding seems to suggest again that the prime interest of *Blanc* is in the intersection between memory and fantasy and the capacity for film as medium to elide the difference between the two. For Karol, memory serves as setting for a form of visual fantasy in which he may re-view his wife and wedding day from different angles in a manner entirely proto-cinematic. It is as if Karol's memory has stored different takes of this scene of his marriage, different virtual representations which he replays at will. That his fantasy or memory may be shared by Dominique need not confirm its objective status, its veracity as visual trace of the events which took place, but may reveal rather her similar investment in a proliferating visual narrative of the union between them.

In these flashbacks, or fantasies, Kieślowski may be seen to explore the set of images which themselves adhere to the concept of a white wedding. The Catholic tradition of France and Poland is comparable here. Kieślowski brings some fairly literal representations of whiteness into his film: the white wedding, white snow, a white statue, white light. Yet haunting the image of the *mariage en blanc* is its almost homonym in French, the *mariage blanc* or unconsummated marriage. As much as the colour is a subject in this film, *Blanc* seems to explore the association between whiteness and blankness, or emptiness, emphasized further in French by the double meaning of the single adjective. Here it is all too significant that Karol's confirmation that his wedding went unconsummated should be heard over the first shots of the white wedding. Effectively the memory or fantasy of the *mariage en blanc* serves both to commemorate and disavow the failure of the *mariage blanc*. The memory appears to replace the failure, to blank it out. That his marriage should be such a gilded memory, so intact in his mind, heightens the loss in its failure, yet also the status of the memory as illusion.

It is telling that the ceremony of marriage, and its failure, is itself so central to the film. Judith Butler comments in her work on performance and performativity: 'The centrality of the marriage ceremony in J. L. Austin's examples of performativity suggests that the heterosexualization of the social bond is the paradigmatic form for those speech acts which bring about what they name. "I pronounce you..." puts into effect the relation that it names.'[38] She continues: 'But from where and when does such a performative draw its force, and what happens to the performative when its purpose is precisely to undo the presumptive force of the heterosexual ceremonial?' The heterosexual ceremony, and a fairly unreconstructed model of heterosexual desire (depending on male potency and female receptive fulfilment), create the infrastructure of *Blanc*. Yet Kieślowski's subject is the initial failure of this ceremony, and, contrary to Austin, the relative impotence of the performative utterance in the face of the failed performance of the body that matters.

Butler, explaining the force of the performative, links its power to its citation, its repeated utterance. For Butler such citation may have given the performative its binding or conferring power, yet the dependence of the performative on repetition, and its very temporality, may open the way for less stabilizing re-articulations of a given discourse or law. Aptly *Blanc* (and much of Kieślowski's filmmaking) appears to put forward the view that repetition always embodies difference (note the two different views of the one marriage flashback). This point might be applied too to Kieślowski's seeming repetition of the structure of viewing relations which predominate in heterosexist narrative cinema. Citation as used so frequently by Kieślowski in cinematic terms may commemorate the source film, but always works also to displace the model, not merely to double or reaffirm it. I would see the constant series of internal references in Kieślowski's films as part of an on-going investigation and displacement of central issues (such as voyeurism and impotence) rather than a circular re-visiting of familiar obsessions.

Kieślowski effectively returns to the model of desiring and viewing relations both constructed and represented in narrative cinema and heterosexual romance. His filmmaking risks appearing outmoded in its treatment of desire, as in his backward glance to the thematics of heterosexual desire and adultery which predominate in *Le Mépris*. Yet his achievement does not lie specifically in retrospection or commemoration. Rather Kieślowski, following Godard, reveals the constructed status of the norm to which he alludes, that norm being cinematic representation of the heterosexual romance. Kieślowski returns to the most familiar place of narrative cinema, and while the viewer finds that she knows that place already and has known it in its multiple other cinematic inscriptions, *Blanc* persuades us nevertheless that this place still differs from itself. Its power relations are by no means easily mapped, as voyeurism finds its couple in exhibitionism; repeated images themselves work to deny the division between virtual and actual, between fantasy and memory trace. For Kieślowski, in *Blanc*, the voyeur can never fully recognize himself, can never fully inhabit the name by which his social identity is inaugurated and mobilized. *Blanc*, like *Le Mépris* ironically, is about the failure of the heterosexual romance in cinema, and about one character's attempts to disavow that failure.

viii Death and Disavowal

In the coda to his book *White* Richard Dyer accounts for the relation he perceives between whiteness and death. He comments: 'The theme of whiteness and death takes many forms.'[39] In elaborating these thoughts he adds the anecdote: 'It is said that when sub-Saharan Africans first saw Europeans, they took them for dead people, for living cadavers.' Dyer's association of death and whiteness depends on associations between pathological states and cadaverous pallor. Yet his interest too is in white as blankness, and its links to death as annihilation. He adds further: 'Death may in some traditions be a vivid experience, but within much of the white tradition it is a blank that may be immateriality (pure spirit) or else just nothing at all.'

Blanc bears no ostensible discourse about whiteness as skin colour or signifier of race. (This may be a lack or limit in the film.) There is, however, a morbid concern with death, blankness and annihilation. Whether these obsessions are specifically linked in the film to the colour which is Kieślowski's symbolic subject is not always clear. Links to notions of equality, invoking the idea of Death as the Great

Leveller, seem more evident, however. From the opening shots of the
trunk resembling a mock coffin, *Blanc* is haunted by signifiers of death
and, most importantly, its disavowal. The trunk is after all only a mock
coffin. The mock deaths of *Blanc* reveal an interest as much in
resurrection as in annihilation. Dave Kehr argues: 'The whiteness of
White—snow, subway tiles, sheets, statuary—suggests an emptiness
that is also a new beginning, a void that might be filled. And so, the
film's emphasis on mock resurrections: Karol unexpectedly climbing
from the coffinlike trunk in which he has been smuggled back from
Poland; Mikołaj's revival in the subway, when he realizes that Karol
has shot him with a blank; and the elaborate scheme (including the
purchase of a Russian corpse) that produces Karol's return from the
dead.'[40] In its interest in resurrection or rebirth, real or otherwise,
Blanc draws close to *Bleu* and its emphasis on survival in denial. The
question of death and disavowal is also linked further, in *Blanc*, to the
issues of voyeurism and futurity which have been our subject.

In *Blanc*, Karol seeks the privilege to witness his own funeral. This
paradoxical position is afforded by his decision to stage his own death
in order to entice Dominique from France to bury him and inherit
his money. Whereas Karol has planned to absent himself from Poland
as the ceremony takes place, in fact he cannot resist the temptation of
a glance which is at once retrospective and anticipatory, the former
because it allows him to re-enter his romance with Dominique, the
latter because it allows him to pre-view his own demise. The scene of
the funeral is staged specifically as scenario of voyeurism.

In the opening of the scene, Karol's face moves gradually into the
frame in a space left between two trees. It is evident that he is
watching something intently: his expression is entirely rapt. The film
cuts to the funeral seen from a distance, with Dominique only just
visible between Mikołaj and Karol's brother, Jurek. The film then cuts
several times between the viewer and the scene viewed until the
funeral is over and Dominique stands alone at the graveside, her head
slightly bowed and her grief apparent. As this image is replaced, music
from the soundtrack slowly wells up and we see Karol raising a small
pair of opera glasses to his face so he can view Dominique's grief in
close-up. We share his vision as the film cuts now to an image of
Delpy's face which all but fills the frame. The camera seems to linger
as the wind blows lightly in her hair, and over the soundtrack,
implausibly, we hear her intake of breath as she weeps. The
subsequent cut to Karol seems to suggest that he has fallen in love

with his ex-wife once more in this moment of voyeurism. The last image of Delpy in this sequence is followed by darkness, the very darkness which will be broken as she opens the door into the hotel bedroom in the scene which is pre-viewed throughout *Blanc*, and which becomes the film's major locus of fantasy and desire.

Karol seeks a vantage point of futurity to witness his own burial. This act of witnessing remains illusory, a deluded product of his desire to master his destiny and its contingency. This desire for mastery is, as we have seen, linked in *Blanc* to the illusory mastery achieved by Metz's voyeur in the cinema. Indeed, *Blanc* shows up this very mastery as a cinematic illusion here in those moments where the viewing of Delpy is rendered self-conscious for the external spectator, as lushly cinematic music plays implausibly through the course of the viewing scenario.

Finally it seems that Karol's success is his failure, that the power he wields over Dominique serves precisely and perversely to preserve his distance from her. This in turn can be explained further with reference again to Žižek. Žižek looks specifically at the theme of a 'disappearance that everybody denies',[41] analysing films which contend with a woman who vanishes. He argues: 'It is difficult not to recognize in this phantomlike figure the apparition of Woman, of the woman who could fill out the lack in man, the ideal partner with whom the sexual relationship would finally be possible, in short, The Woman who, according to Lacanian theory, precisely does not exist.' It is Dominique's absence from his life that Karol has denied, it is his belief in the possibility and ideal of their sexual relationship that he has perpetuated. Žižek explains: 'The Other Woman is prohibited insofar as she "does not exist"; she is mortally dangerous because of the ultimate discord between her fantasy figure and the "empirical" woman who, quite by chance, finds herself occupying this fantasy place.' It is this discord, interestingly acknowledged and analysed in *Le Mépris*, that Karol seeks to disavow. Both *Le Mépris* and *Blanc* offer their own response to Žižek's Lacanian intimation that 'the power of fascination exerted by a sublime image always announces a lethal dimension'. According to Žižek: 'It is only when the poet loses his lady that he finally and truly acquires her, it is precisely through this loss that she gains her place in the fantasy space that regulates the subject's desire.'

It is through her incarceration, rather than death, that Dominique gains her ultimate place in the fantasy space that regulates Karol's desires. Kieślowski appears in the first instance to stop short of the final acknowledgement that in the cinema, and in the psyche, loss regulates desire. His subject is the disavowal of that loss. Here prison affords the stasis to preserve the *idée fixe* of Dominique, or Delpy as 'la Femme'. Where it seemed that Karol's death and its re-staging were the subject of the film, we emerge ultimately with the sense that in his fake demise he is in every sense equalled by Dominique whose absence is preserved spatially while denied psychologically in the ending of the film.

As we saw previously, Karol seeks to deny contingency in his search for control over causality. The flashforwards of the film represent in part his manic attempts to choreograph his life, to stage it, ironically, like a film. Yet his existence is bound by the limits of this attempt. On one level, as in *Bleu*, Kieślowski appears to affirm the success of disavowal and denial. Karol denies his loss of Dominique and succeeds in restoring her to himself as object of desire. But this is effectively at the expense of his annihilation and hers, in different ways. His disavowal leads him, at the end of the film, to be the dupe of a cinematic illusion and to assume once again a masochistic position as he is the victim of the losses of his own desire. Dominique is forever absent to him. I have argued that Kieślowski makes us re-think voyeurism and its power structures. This is certainly one of the achievements of *Blanc* and a feature which links it to the unobtrusive self-reflexivity of much of Kieślowski's work. The final ethical wager of *Blanc* is to reveal the very pleasures and delusions which may derive from a desire to pursue an existence fostered by cinematic illusion. This investigation with identification, and its fault-lines, is pursued, with more gravity, in the final part of the trilogy, Kieślowski's last film.

Notes to Chapter 3

1. Karol's name is the Polish equivalent of Charlie. This name, and the nature of the character, have been linked to Charlie Chaplin. Karol is played by Zbigniew Zamachowski who, despite the pathos of his acting, can be associated with the blackly comic aspects of Kieślowski's filmmaking. This is evident in his role as Artur in *Decalogue 10*.

2. Delpy incarnates a blonde ideal of French femininity, appearing as the progeny of Bardot and Deneuve. She first appeared on screen in Godard's *Détective* (1984). More recently she has appeared in US productions, notably playing the part of Céline, a young French student, in Richard Linklater's *Before Sunrise* (1994). This film, with its implied references to Rivette's *Céline et Julie vont en bateau* (1974), seems fascinated by the French cinema of Rivette, Rohmer and Truffaut and,

despite its setting in Vienna, uses the body, image and voice of Delpy as a reminder of its love of this tradition.

3. On the re-release of *Le Mépris* in the UK in 1996, Colin MacCabe commented: 'In many ways *Le Mépris* is Jean-Luc Godard's most orthodox movie, with a best selling novel, a star cast, the largest budget he ever worked with, and a relatively developed narrative. But the film is also as cinematically adventurous as any other by Godard.' *Sight and Sound* 6/9 (Sept. 1996), 55–6, 55.

4. Jean-Luc Godard, *Le Mépris*, *L'Avant-scène cinéma* 412/413 (May/June 1992), 13.

5. Of course, Kieślowski dwells further on the relation between an advertising poster and the stilled frame of a film in *Trois Couleurs: Rouge*. In a feature on marketing in a recent edition of *Sight and Sound* Justin Wyatt comments on the posters used to market the trilogy: 'For art-house films that fall outside generic boundaries, successful marketing often shifts to more basic strategies: for Kieślowski's trilogy *Three Colours Blue*, *White* and *Red* (1993), genre, storyline and thematics were ignored in favour of large, artfully sexy images of Juliette Binoche, Irène Jacob and Julie Delpy against the colour of the title each appeared in.' 'Sight and Sound A–Z of Cinema: M Marketing', *Sight and Sound* 7/6 (June 1997), 38–41. This may reflect the marketing strategies used in the USA and the UK, but overlooks the fact that on the first release of *Blanc* in France, a close-up image of Zbigniew Zamachowski was used, with a smaller superimposed image of Delpy in the background. Further, the commercialization of the image such marketing represents might be seen precisely as one of Kieślowski's subjects in his exploration of capitalism in *Blanc* and advertising in *Rouge*.

6. As Ginette Vincendeau reminds us: 'She was idolized—her gingham dresses, hairstyle and pout were copied by millions of women, and she modelled for the effigy of the French Republic—but also viciously attacked and abused.' *The Companion to French Cinema* (London, 1996), 26. Beauvoir offers an analysis of this ambivalence to Bardot in *Brigitte Bardot and the Lolita Syndrome*. Here she seeks to explain, amongst other things, Bardot's greater appeal abroad than in France. This well-documented phenomenon may sit rather oddly with my use of Bardot here to represent the *French* film icon of femininity for Kieślowski. I would add, however, that it is as such that she is re-viewed in *Le Mépris* by Godard, and that it is as such that she is viewed precisely outside France. And *Blanc* in many ways might be seen to dramatize the outsider's view of France, both psychologically and cinematically, for both Kieślowski and his protagonist.

7. As we find noted in the screenplay, for this scene, 'un filtre rouge uniformise les couleurs' (Godard, *Le Mépris*, 15). Godard's use of a filter here might be compared to Kieślowski's more lavish use of golden filter in *La Double Vie de Véronique* to create again an aura of intimacy and eroticism which, for Godard, is quickly undermined.

8. In the film's dialogue, Camille's voice echoes insistently, like a child: 'Tu vois mes pieds dans la glace [...] Tu vois mon derrière dans la glace?' (Godard, *Le Mépris*, 15).

9. Nicole Brenez, 'Cinématographie du figurable', in Godard, *Le Mépris*, 1–9, 7.

10. The term 'fracture of the icon' is used here in part to anticipate the literal shattering of an icon of femininity, the plaster bust of a young girl which Karol steals to become an effigy of Dominique. Notably, after this icon has been smashed, Karol manages to glue it back together.

11. Laura Mulvey, *Fetishism and Curiosity* (London, 1996), 88.

12. Danusia Stok (ed.), *Kieślowski on Kieślowski* (London, 1993), 250.

13. Bernard Bénoliel, 'Krzysztof Kieślowski: souvenirs de Pologne', *Cahiers du cinéma* 515 (July/Aug. 1997), 9.

14. Scorsese's *Casino* (1995), a film which at least in its soundtrack makes reference to *Le Mépris*, also associates voyeurism and surveillance specifically as Ace (Robert de Niro) watches Ginger (Sharon Stone) on the video monitor of a surveillance system, mingling paranoia and desire. Surveillance itself (now auditory, not visual) is of course a prime subject in *Trois Couleurs: Rouge* as the Judge monitors his neighbour's voices, lives and interference.

15. Stok (ed.), *Kieślowski on Kieślowski*, 169. In speaking about Szapołowska as an 'enigmatic blonde woman' I am perhaps being disingenuous since in some shots her hair appears an ordinary mid-brown. Yet it is noticeable that in the interior sequences of the film, both those viewed voyeuristically by Tomek and those in which he also is present (in a café eating ice cream and in Magda's apartment when she attempts to seduce him) her hair is lit in such a way as to be suffused with golden reflections and fairly luminescent. Szapołowska is here in part reminiscent of Domiziana Giordano who plays Eugenia in Tarkovsky's *Nostalghia* (1983).

16. The touch of Magda's thighs and her words telling him that she is wet inside have more than the desired effect on Tomek. His premature ejaculation seems linked to the series of images of spilt milk which run through the film. Notably in *Blanc* Dominique divorces Karol because, despite his love for her, he cannot consummate their marriage.

17. In the television film, Tomek survives to return to the post office and to rebuff Magda who now regrets her earlier mockery of his ideals. In the bleaker feature-length version, Tomek's suicide is successful.

18. Carol Clover, *Men, Women and Chainsaws: Gender in the Modern Horror Film* (London, 1992), 204, 204.

19. Williams, *Viewing Positions*.

20. Laura Mulvey, 'Visual Pleasure and Narrative Cinema', in *Feminism and Film*, ed. Constance Penley (London, 1988), 57–68, 68.

21. Aptly Kieślowski literally takes difficulties in translation as his subject (here again echoing *Le Mépris*). Karol is shown to have a poor command of French. An interpreter is used in his divorce hearing; he fears this may limit his freedom of speech. In a poignant scene back in Warsaw, he is seen to be working on his French with the use a French language tape which repeats back to him the forms of the imperfect subjunctive of the verb 'plaire': of course 'que je plusse' offers a close indication of Karol's desire. Once he has caught Dominique in the trap of his love and brought her to Poland, she in turn stumbles in a foreign language and becomes enmeshed in the legal system, as Karol was a victim in France.

22. This parity is founded in part on the film's focus on the ways in which the economy and society of Poland are becoming copies or doubles of Western Europe.

23. Metz, *Psychoanalysis and Cinema*, 60, 60.

24. The Palais de Justice on the Ile de la cité in Paris has the words *LIBERTE EGALITE FRATERNITE* emblazoned across its parapet. The building is the

point of intersection and interference between *Bleu* and *Blanc* as Julie, in the former film, stumbles into Karol's divorce hearing. This scene is viewed in both films, but from a different perspective.

25. The relation between virtuality and futurity is evidently very complex. Elizabeth Grosz has begun exploring such issues in a paper, 'Deleuze, Bergson and uncharted futures: duration, the virtual and history'. I am very grateful to her for giving me a copy of this. Grosz's emphasis here is on the possibility of speculation about the future and of reconstituting memory as a form of production. In this sense her engaged analysis differs somewhat from my own interest in the relation between futurity, fate and wish-fulfilment as embroiled in the temporality of cinematic narrative.

26. Deleuze, *Cinéma 2*, 72.

27. Metz, *Psychoanalysis and Cinema*, 63.

28. This image, and its repetition, is reminiscent of the virtual image of herself which Magda watches in the coda to *A Short Film about Love*. The connection between the scenes seems to rest on the contiguity of subject matter, and equally on their comparable virtuality. (Opening a door and entering a new space appears as an apt image of interconnectedness and interference.)

29. Kehr, 'To Save the World'.

30. Slavoj Žižek, *Looking Awry: An Introduction to Jacques Lacan through Popular Culture* (Cambridge, MA, 1991), 69, 69, 70, 70.

31. Kieślowski, *Decalogue*, p. ix.

32. In this chapter of *Looking Awry*, 'How the Non-duped Err', Žižek makes use of questions of illusory and reverse teleology in popular culture to offer a reading of the Lacanian thesis: 'the big Other does not exist'. He explains as follows: 'The big Other does not exist as subject of history; it is not given in advance and does not regulate our activity in a teleological way. Teleology is always a retroactive illusion...' (78).

33. In this scene Dominique is seen silhouetted and then the window goes dark, as if she has switched off the light, only to be illuminated once more as the shadows of two figures are now seen and Karol realizes she is sleeping with someone else. A similar sequence of images, where the light is switched on and off, is found already in *A Short Film about Love* where Magda stages Tomek's scene of voyeurism, disclosing to her lover that they are being watched. Interpreting these scenes in tandem emphasizes the ways in which Dominique, like Magda, is in part in control of the viewing relations which circulate around her image. Yet Magda here works arguably to short-circuit such desires, where Dominique's role as exhibitionist, contrarily, will prove crucial to my reading of *Blanc*.

34. Metz, *Psychoanalysis and Cinema*, 60.

35. Kieślowski, *Trois Couleurs* II, 12.

36. This comment is itself in part motivated by Freud's visual image of wish fulfilment in 'Creative Writers and Day-dreaming' where he writes: 'Just as, in many altar-pieces, the portrait of the donor is to be seen in a corner of the picture, so, in the majority of ambitious phantasies, we can discover in some corner or other the lady for whom the creator of the phantasy performs all his heroic deeds and at whose feet all his triumphs are laid.' *Penguin Freud Library 14. Art and Literature* (London, 1985), 135.

37. Metz, *Psychoanalysis and Cinema*, 63, 73.
38. Judith Butler, *Bodies that Matter: On the Discursive Limits of Sex* (London, 1993), 224, 224–5.
39. Richard Dyer, *White* (London, 1997), 208, 209, 207.
40. Kehr, 'To Save the World', 13.
41. Žižek, *Looking Awry*, 79, 80, 83, 83, 86.

CHAPTER 4

❖

Identification and Disaster
Trois Couleurs: Rouge

1 Disaster Movie

Trois Couleurs: Rouge has proved to be the end of Kieślowski's film-making. With the film's completion in 1994, Kieślowski publicly announced the end of his career and his desire to devote his life to more contemplative activities.[1] This decision was overtaken by a heart attack in August 1995 and the director's premature death in March 1996. The viewer is left now with two possible conclusions to Kieślowski's career. Rumour had it, at Cannes in 1995, that Kieślowski's retirement was abortive and that the director was considering a resurrection in his career in order to create a further trilogy on the subjects of Heaven, Hell and Purgatory, of, we may imagine, all the more epic proportions. Journalists and critics confirm that Kieślowski had signed a contract to co-write this project.[2] Yet this intimation of futurity appears undermined by the manifold ways in which *Rouge*, as a last film, offers a sense of an ending and its own internal discourse on direction, vicarious existence and closure itself. Giving the viewer the possibly illusory signal that his series of films is now complete, Kieślowski necessarily prepares us for a present moment of reckoning and recollection. *Rouge* provides a sense of an ending which can only be understood by retracing the steps of Kieślowski's previous films and isolating the themes of necessity, free will and pure chance which recur at every turn.

Rouge offers an admirably equivocal ending to a career, a still point in a director's history of moving pictures. Readings of this 'final' film have almost entirely privileged notions of humanity, hope and redemption. It will be my aim here to contest this construction of a positive and redemptive teleology, and to challenge the now recurrent view of Kieślowski as humanist (despite my interest in the human dimension of his work).

Critics have been keen to perceive a positive development in Kieślowski's ethical and aesthetic position. Agnès Peck claims: 'Le pessimisme antérieur de Kieślowski semble s'inverser dans la trilogie.'[3] She suggests that Kieślowski offers his viewers 'un humanisme actuel, éloigné du moralisme et de l'idéologie, qui témoigne d'un sens aigu de la relativité et de l'ambiguïté, et questionne le spectateur sur notre époque'. For Kehr, *Rouge* serves well to restore and redeem the faltering images of humanity in Kieślowski's earlier films: hence Kehr's interest in the image of the old woman struggling to deposit her bottle in a bottle bank which recurs through *La Double Vie de Véronique* and the trilogy. Kehr describes the scene: 'Valentine, as she leaves the theatre near the end of *Red*, sees the old woman struggling and stops to help her, reaching up to drop the bottle in its slot.'[4] Kehr claims: 'In a sense that single, simple act of kindness is the climax of the entire trilogy, the gesture that saves the world.' In Kehr's final judgement on *Rouge* as film of redemption, he writes: 'The Judge is the first of the trilogy's characters to see someone beyond himself; for Kieślowski, all the hope for the world resides in that fact.' I have less faith in Kieślowski's belief in hope, as evidenced in his later cinema.

Philip Kemp suggests that a redemptive reading may risk erring on the side of superficiality. He expands on the possibilities of a more sceptical interpretation of the film: '*Red* ostensibly rounds off the whole trilogy with a neat happy ending, but the closer one looks at it the more ironies obtrude. For a start, just how "happy" is it for 1400 to drown so that two strangers can meet? And can we assume from that final freeze-frame of Auguste and Valentine that they'll fall in love, or even notice each other? Kern may want to think so and so may we, but there's precious little evidence for the idea. Kieślowski goes further, piling on the implausibilities: both couples from *Blue* and *White* turn up among the survivors—as if to mock our desire for a cosily romantic conclusion.'[5] Kemp concludes: '*Red* starts to unravel backwards—or rather to re-ravel into a different pattern.'

It is certainly difficult to reconcile the idea of this seeming 'happy' ending with the full horror of the major tragedy the film represents. This representation becomes ethically questionable when one sees how closely this tragedy, which serves the purposes of Kieślowski's fiction so well, resembles the real event of the Zeebrugge ferry disaster. Such a resemblance seems more disturbing in the face of glancing similarities between *Rouge* and the genre of the disaster movie. Further, we may question whether a director as subtle and as pessimistic as Kieślowski will allow his trilogy to end with the coincidence and trite conclusion ensuring the freak survival of those characters whose destinies the viewer has followed. Even if such a confected ending merely worked to mock the viewer's desire for resolution, as Kemp suggests, surely the viewer would feel in some sense cheated by virtue of the very divergence of this 'final' film from the path taken by its more opaque and doubting predecessors?

As I have been suggesting throughout, rather than offering a happy resolution the trilogy ends, appropriately, in blind chance.[6] This one scene of survival is, as I have argued, the necessary catalyst for the trilogy as a whole: it is not so much its culmination as its cause, as Kieślowski reflects the films' inception in their closing. As Sobociński, the film's cinematographer, reveals, this precedence of the ending was quite literal, at least in the shooting of *Rouge*: 'We had shot the last scene of the film, the video "news footage" of the ferry-boat accident, several months before we began principal photography.'[7] As gradually appears obvious to the viewer, the lives and locations of the protagonists of the three parts of the trilogy are barely related, despite the internal references and visual stylization of Kieślowski's filmmaking. Kieślowski himself comments: '*Blue*, *White* and *Red* are three individual films, three separate films. Of course they were made to be shown in this order but that doesn't mean that you can't watch them the other way round. There were a lot of connections between the films of the *Decalogue*. There are fewer connections here and they're far less important.'[8] Critics have chosen both implicitly and explicitly to disagree with Kieślowski's claims for the discon-nectedness of his films. The aim inherent in various projects, and in part in my own, to re-read the trilogy through the filter offered by its ending in *Rouge*, necessarily makes a claim for interrelation in practice if not in theory. But if blind chance is Kieślowski's dominant theme, then disconnectedness is essential to the credible survival of these three narrative films.

As viewers we are offered the chance, and meaningless, survival of a handful of strangers. At the moment of their survival, as we witness it, the only links between the lives of the protagonists of the separate films are tenuous, metaphorical or emphatically cinematic. Inasmuch as we are persuaded to view these lives as potentially parallel destinies, the only point of literal convergence in their destinies in the diegesis of the trilogy, besides the ferry disaster, is the entrance of Julie in *Bleu* into the court scene in *Blanc* (viewed from different angles in the two films). Where a door is momentarily opened between the films, it is closed as quickly, as Julie discovers that she is intruding on the trial in process. Beyond this, and the ending, the parallels between their destinies are obviously completely unknown to the protagonists of the separate films: they are strangers to one another, not neighbours as in *Decalogue*.

Kieślowski's ultimate lesson in *Rouge* is not simply one of hope and redemption (although many viewers concur that this is Kieślowski's most tender film), but one, once again, of chance and betrayal.[9] *Rouge* works, I think, to reveal to the viewer ways in which the cinematic medium may operate to disrupt our processing of visual evidence. What we find in Kieślowski's films is not merely a pessimistic and ultimately fatalistic interpretation of the human condition, but also a profound lack of faith in the capacity of the photographic image, and its montage in film, to bear witness to the vicissitudes of an individual destiny. In this sense, throughout his films, and all the more insistently in *Rouge*, Kieślowski places the role of the film director in question, and places his authority under erasure. Kieślowski allows his viewers no confidence in the capacity of the cinematic medium to gain access to the real: yet this is perpetually a cause of distress rather than re-evaluation in his films up to and culminating in *Rouge*. I believe, reluctantly perhaps, that it is unduly optimistic to suppose that this fissure in the façade of Kieślowski's filmmaking has been filled and closed in the final part of his trilogy.

II Prospero and Miranda

Rouge is in many senses a film about return. Where *Bleu* revealed the trauma of a return to the mother's house, now an empty echo chamber, a *maison de retraite*, *Rouge* stages the return to the father's house, a return prefigured at the end of *La Double Vie de Véronique*, and a return overdetermined in significance in Kieślowski's filmmaking. Valentine enters the Judge's house to find it a house of spectres, haunted by the voices of the surrounding neighbourhood. It is a house of memories, of the permanent presence of the past. In this house she finds the retired Judge, *un juge à la retraite*, a melancholy Prospero who treats her with indifference.

As viewers, we first encounter the Judge from Valentine's perspective, both psychologically and visually. In a random road accident (a catalyst of action as in *Bleu*) Valentine knocks down and injures a German shepherd dog. True to her role throughout the film, her impulses are humanitarian and reparative. She takes the dog carefully in her arms and lays it in her car, then looking at its identity tag so she can restore it to its owner. The camera closes in on her finger, slightly stained by the dog's blood, as, like Véronique or Julie, she traces out the path she will take on a map to reach what we will see become the Judge's house. It is dark and we see from the lights glistening on the road that it has been raining: throughout *Rouge* the weather is resolutely overcast and blustery. Valentine pauses for some while at the Judge's gate. We see that the windows of the house are illuminated, but there is darkness all around. As Valentine decides to enter through the gate, to cross the threshold into the Judge's house, we watch her from a distance as she walks up the path, her figure now lit by the reflected light from the windows. At a distance we hear her hollow knock on the door. The film cuts to a close-up of her face framed in a pane of the glass door, pensive, slightly anxious, and precisely as she might be viewed from the interior of the house. The film then cuts to a disquieting sequence of images where we find, in a visual allusion to *La Double Vie de Véronique*, a series of forwards tracking shots with a handheld camera exploring the spaces of the house as Valentine enters its dimensions. The camera appears literally to inhabit her body. The viewer is offered a lurching approach to the space of the Judge's fantasy, and his desires, as our whole perspective tilts with Valentine's echoing footsteps as she walks down the empty passageways. The set seems literally to evolve around Valentine as a glass door swings open, as lights draw the attention of this embodied gaze on either side. A further disorientation is achieved, however, as Valentine herself seems to step into her own field of vision, as her figure comes into our view on screen right. The seemingly complete accord between her gaze and ours is disrupted and we then watch her continue into the Judge's study where her gaze and the camera's coincide once more as his seated, sleeping figure is drawn more closely into focus. The viewer quickly learns that this will be a space of distorted perception, and of illusion.

This distortion of sense impressions is enhanced by the eerie noises which emanate from the Judge's study and appear at first extra-diegetic. We hear the whine of radio waves and their tuneless distortions. The viewer may remember that this very sound is heard, with verisimilitude, as Valentine sits in her car in the moments before she runs down the dog Rita who will lead her into this new space in her destiny. The sound of the radio waves, which holds the status, almost, of an aural flashforward for the viewer, marks Valentine's entry into the Judge's orbit and the illusory circle of his power. She enters as an intruder, her first words apologizing and explaining that the door was left open. The house is permeable, with no stable relation between inside and out. It houses the elements, it seems. The barriers which Valentine must cross as she enters, where we see her pausing, are psychological rather than physical, mental and possibly temporal.

In the study she finds the Judge surrounded by disordered books and papers, a veritable library. It appears that he is sleeping and she wakes him, shocks him almost into consciousness. Valentine must seem as much the stuff of his dream as of his reality. Her words explain the accident and he turns to look at her, all response to her seemingly muted. Here a shot/reverse shot sequence separates Valentine and the Judge spatially and presents the image of each to the other. The Judge's face is seen in profile outlined by rim lighting as he seems now to ignore and deny any emotional response to Valentine's revelation. His attitude is one of pure thought and measured consideration. She proceeds, in defiance, to voice the words which are effectively the central wager of the film and which provide us with evidence to suggest that this scene itself is pivotal in the film as a whole.

Shocked by the Judge's lack of response to her narration of the road accident, Valentine asks: 'Si j'avais écrasé votre fille, ça vous ferait le même effet?'[10] The Judge replies, with just logic: 'Je n'ai pas de fille, mademoiselle.' The Judge has looked up at Valentine as he speaks these words. He now resumes his position in profile and in contemplation as he curtly tells Valentine to leave, turns entirely away from her and shouts after her not to close the door. As Valentine promptly exits from the Judge's house, again a forwards tracking shot takes us for an instant towards the solitude of the Judge's study, before the film cuts to Valentine emerging from the lighted house into the darkness. Almost imperceptibly here we view the Judge coming to the window to watch her leave unobserved. She appears to sense his presence as she turns at the gate, movement in the lighted window catching her eye. The film cuts then to the clean space of the veterinarian's, oddly reminiscent of the clinic in *Bleu* where Julie learns to recover and forget.

In this first scene with the Judge, Valentine enters an enchanted realm. Kieślowski in his last film pays tribute to Shakespeare's last play and its imbrication of fantasy and physicality. The Judge, as I have implied, is a modern, melancholy Prospero. He sits in his library as in a cell. His house is filled, like Prospero's island, with the sounds of spirits. Here we might recall Caliban's words:

> Be not afeard; the isle is full of noises,
> Sounds, and sweet airs, that give delight and hurt not.
> Sometimes a thousand twangling instruments
> Will hum about mine ears; and sometime voices
> That, if I then had waked after long sleep,
> Will make me sleep again; and then, in dreaming,
> The clouds methought would open, and show riches
> Ready to drop upon me, that when I waked
> I cried to dream again.   (III. ii. 136–44)

Kieślowski too seems to disturb the boundary between dream and reality, between virtual and actual in this his last film. If the Judge is Prospero, testing vengeance, wielding his supernatural powers and lamenting his mortality, Valentine is his Miranda. Yet she is only ever a virtual daughter.

The theatrical intertext gives a sign, it seems, of the nature of Valentine's relation to the Judge, and of the role she must play. Prospero's own love for Miranda, as witnessed in the play, appears to traverse the paternal to become all but romantic. Speaking of Ferdinand, indeed, he calls Miranda 'his and mine loved darling' (III. iii. 94), the very proximity of the possessive adjectives indicating the equivalence of sentiment and tie. Valentine is for the Judge more than a daughter and less than a lover: she is the woman he would have loved, as Kieślowski dwells on the pained intimations of the conditional perfect tense. Valentine is also the daughter whom he did not have, as her presence seems to jar unduly with the Judge's statement of his own childless state. Most properly she is the existential test delivered to him, the witness to his life who will allow him to determine what his love for a daughter might have been.

Paternal/filial love has a special place in Kieślowski's filmmaking. It is the haven of *La Double Vie de Véronique* and its locus of safety.[11] Elsewhere in Kieślowski's filmmaking, however, this love seems associated with fear of loss. In *Decalogue 1* that loss is too painfully literal as the father confronts the loss of his beloved son in a skating accident. In *Decalogue 4* that loss is more complex as doubts over paternity give rise to the possibility of the loss of a daughter in her discovery as an object of desire. Both these films seem relevant to

Rouge where the Judge's love for his virtual daughter appears to go on trial as he recognizes, yet renounces, the object of desire she might have been, and faces the enormity of her loss in his fear that she is a victim in the ferry disaster, the tempest his fantasy has provoked. The ending of the film, which in a sense I discuss continually in this chapter, offers its own answer to Valentine's question. The Judge's response to the loss of a daughter, hypothetical in Valentine's question, and virtual in the role she plays in the Judge's life, is by now, we may assume, unequivocal. His pain is very real. The film has effectively proved that relation.

III The Law of the Father

If the Judge becomes, as I have argued, a virtual father, he is necessarily by virtue of his profession a literal as well as symbolic guardian of the law. Yet Kieślowski's filmmaking is far from paternalistic in its relation to the law.

In the figure of the Judge, Kieślowski allows the concerns of his Polish and French cinema to coalesce. Since his collaboration with Krzysztof Piesiewicz, the lawyer who co-scripted *No End*, *Decalogue* and the trilogy, Kieślowski has used a literal and metaphoric legal system as infrastructure in his cinema. The central building and space of interference in the trilogy is, after all, the Palais de Justice in Paris. Lawyers and legal judgements recur in Kieślowski's films as he seems again and again to attempt to resolve questions about liability, volition and fatality. He constructs his ethical system which remains resolutely subjective, even existential in bias.

It becomes clear in *A Short Film about Killing*, arguably Kieślowski's finest film and one which bears many echoes which resonate in *Rouge*, that for Kieślowski the guardians of the legal system are themselves as much on trial as the perpetrators of crimes whose actions they attempt to judge. As Žižek brilliantly sums up *A Short Film about Killing*:

This rendering of the machinery of law at work is so disturbing because it registers the *failure of the 'metaphor of Law,'* that is, of the metaphoric substitution of the punishment for the crime: the punishment is not experienced as just retribution that undoes the harm brought about by the crime, but rather as its uncanny repetition—the act of punishment is somehow tainted by an additional obscenity that makes it a travesty, an obscene repetition of the original crime in the guise of law.[12]

In these terms the place and gravity of the legal system in Kieślowski's filmmaking is by no means certain. The concerns of Piotr, the young lawyer in *A Short Film about Killing*, seem central to the moral anxiety which, I argue, pervades Kieślowski's work not merely in the 1980s but into the 1990s.

Piotr, as much as Jacek, is on trial in *A Short Film about Killing*. His destiny parallels that of the man whose life he will defend in the film's diegesis, as he himself comments when he remarks that he was in the same bar as Jacek in the very moments when Jacek was winding around his hand the rope which became his murder weapon. Piotr questions whether he could have done something. His question relates symbolically both to the past moment when any action of his might have arrested the course of the destiny which becomes inevitable, and also to his present actions in the court where he attempts, impossibly, to defend Jacek against the death penalty. After the trial Piotr goes to the Judge who has presided and asks if another lawyer or a different defence might have made a difference. The Judge's words are reassuringly categorical, maintaining to Piotr that his was the best argument against the death sentence that he has heard in years, that the verdict was inevitable. The Judge absolves Piotr in words which are absent from the published screenplay, but which are spoken variously in the television and feature-length version of the film: 'You were faultless as a lawyer and as a human being.' This appears to be the verdict Piotr craves in the trial of his own actions. It does not quite bring absolution yet, as the pathos of his regret for Jacek pervades the latter parts of the film.

For Kieślowski, as *A Short Film about Killing* illustrates, the legal system becomes an apparatus for testing personal ethics, and the power of an individual over a specific destiny. This is the system, both legal and cinematic, which is crucial to our understanding of the Judge in *Rouge*. The Judge's history, which he passes in review in his mind in his confessional dialogues with Valentine, is a series of legal judgments, of trial and decision. The courthouse seems the permanent stage of his mental scenarios. He first speaks of his experience as a judge to Valentine when they drink pear brandy together, after she has come to his house on reading of his conviction in court for telephone espionage. He reminisces that on this day, at almost the same hour, some thirty-five years ago, he acquitted a man, a sailor. He says that it was one of his first serious cases and that he was at a difficult time in his own life. Some time later he discovered that he had made a mistake and that the man was guilty. There is a pause in his narration during which, in the increasing darkness of the room, he attempts to put on the light, but the bulb blows immediately. After a few moments he screws in a new bulb, which dazzles Valentine at first, but then gently illuminates her face. All too graphically, we have an image of insight and revelation. The interruption of the narration serves to replace Valentine: she is now placed as judge of the Judge's actions and she passes her verdict on his reminiscence. She asks what happened to the acquitted man and the Judge explains that he made his own investigation to find that the man had married, had three children and that finally (in words which do not appear in the screenplay) 'il vit en paix'. Valentine's face is radiant with this knowledge and she acknowledges to the Judge: 'Vous avez fait ce qu'il fallait.'[13] She continues: 'et même très bien'. She explains to him further, in terms of unusual certainty: 'Vous l'avez sauvé.' Here the theme of redemption, which is itself on trial throughout *Rouge*, comes explicitly to the fore.

Redemption and its responsibilities trouble the Judge, however, as he now makes clear to Valentine. He asks her a question which must remain all but rhetorical: 'combien d'autres est-ce que j'aurais pu acquitter?' How many guilty men could he acquit and save like this? He passes his own judgment on the burden of legal decision, saying: 'le seul sentiment de décider ce qui est la vérité et ce qui ne l'est pas... Maintenant, je pense que c'est un manque de modestie.' The system of Kieślowski's cinema appears to depend on the figure of the father, the figure of the Judge, as witnessed in the themes of his visual narratives and his very authorial stance in his filmmaking. Yet in *Rouge*, Kieślowski questions most thoroughly the failure of such a figure, the avowal of his loss of omnipotence despite his bid for omniscience. *Rouge* allows an individual to confront his own inability to control the destinies which surround him. In this sense, effectively, Kieślowski counterpoints existence and its cinematic representation. He demonstrates the illusion of control the cinematic medium affords, its inherent disavowal of randomness and contingency. Yet he uses this illusory mastery of the visual, of motor control and of personal destiny, in order precisely to reveal the loss of such possibilities in existence itself. In these terms Kieślowski poses existential questions, yet underlines the inadequacy of his cinematic answers. *Rouge* is a film about the failure of vision, and the failure of illusion. It courts the viewer's faith in order to demonstrate its very vanity.

IV Auguste

The desire for omnipotence and its illusory satisfaction is witnessed in one of the major points of coincidence, resistance and inexplicability in the narrative. This concerns the Judge's destiny and the possibilities for its re-viewing and revision. Just as Véronique realizes within her film that she is not alone, but is shadowed by the seemingly cinematic presence of her image, her double self, so the Judge in *Rouge*, we apprehend, is shadowed by his younger double. In this cinematic illusion Kieślowski realizes the tantalizing desire to see an image of the self, but younger, to catch a glimpse of who one was and how one might have been. In real terms, such a desire can only have any semblance of satisfaction photographically through still images, home videos and film. For Kieślowski, as I have suggested, the privilege of narrative cinema is in its potential to visualize parallel destinies, to actualize so many virtual existences. This is the privilege which takes Kieślowski across the bounds of generational difference, allowing the Judge to see himself as a younger man.

Where the Judge releases anecdotes of his first judgments, the film counterpoints his legal position with that of Auguste, whose life intersects tantalizingly with Valentine's as they live as neighbours but unknown to each other for large parts of the film. We hear his failed telephone calls, crosscut with Valentine's, but know nothing at first of his identity. Auguste, as cinematic protagonist, appears in some senses to be an undeveloped copy of Piotr in *A Short Film about Killing*. He too is in the liminal stages of his legal career. Auguste is presented to the viewer both intimately and anonymously. His identity as a law student emerges as he is seen to drop several law books in the street and the camera closes in on the words of the *Droit pénal*. One book has opened at a certain page which, within the coincidences of Kieślowski's filmmaking, holds the answer to a question which Auguste is asked in his final exam. This Auguste reveals to his blonde girlfriend as he emerges from the exam hall.

Later in *Rouge* the Judge attends a fashion show at Valentine's invitation and they speak together in the empty theatre after the show. The Judge reveals that although Valentine could not see him, he sat in his usual seat, a seat where he once sat as a young man, as a law student, where once before his final exams he let his books fall to the floor and found his books open at the very page he needed in his later exams. The repetition speaks for itself. Looking beyond overt cinematic coincidence, I suggest that Kieślowski seeks here a cinematic means for thinking the temporality of identity in his medium and in experience.

Our experience as viewers is at first uncanny. The Judge's words recall a scene we have viewed. We have already seen a virtual representation, a seeming re-enactment of an event which the Judge now claims as a memory and as part of the narrative of his own past history. In this sense we are allowed to know the Judge's memories before they are narrated and to recognize them as they are voiced to Valentine. This process of uncanny recognition is pursued further as the Judge narrates a love story, his love for a blonde woman who betrayed him, whose body he sees reflected in a mirror making love with another man. This scene is again familiar to us as we have seen Auguste making this same painful discovery of infidelity as he watches his girlfriend through a lighted window. We are left with the problem of how to make sense of the uncanny resemblances between the destinies of Auguste and the Judge in *Rouge*.

On one level Kieślowski presents a peculiar contamination between the past histories of particular individuals. This is apt from a director who offers the following narrative of his own relation to the past and to memory:

There are many events in my life which I believe to be a part of my life and yet I don't really know whether or not they happened to me. I think I remember these events very accurately but perhaps this is because somebody else has talked about them. In other words I appropriate incidents from other people's lives. I often don't even remember who I've appropriated or stolen them from. I steal them and then start to believe that they happened to me.[14]

Kieślowski highlights the permeability of memory, and the literal intrusion of other narratives into one's own past history. Yet he seems to explore more than this in *Rouge*. He has stated: 'The theme of *Red* is the conditional mood—what would have happened if the Judge had been born forty years later.' He continues: 'Everything that happens to Auguste happened to the Judge, though, perhaps, slightly differently', and he guides his viewer to ask the following questions: 'So, does Auguste really exist or doesn't he? Is Auguste repeating exactly the Judge's life? Is it possible to repeat somebody's life after some time or not?'

The Judge's relation to Auguste is explored in the film primarily through the role of mediator and object of desire played by Valentine.

Valentine intrudes into the Judge's life; she represents the woman he might have loved, the daughter he might have lost. The reality of the Judge's desire for Valentine is always kept at one remove both spatially and temporally. When the Judge speaks to Valentine of the affective in his life after his betrayal by the blonde woman, he explains that he has been alone perhaps because he hasn't met her, Valentine. Her absence from his life is not repaired, given the forty-year gap between them: rather than seeking to possess her literally it seems that the Judge seeks instead virtual knowledge of Valentine and retrospective satisfaction of his desire. In the scene in the theatre the Judge narrates the details of a dream he has had. In this dream he sees her at 50 and he sees that she is happy. She wakes up in the dream and smiles at someone next to her. In the Judge's narration he tells her that he does not know who is beside her. This empty space is filled doubly in the film. It is filled by the Judge in his desire for Valentine, now replaced by her own image at an age at which he might love her. Yet the space is filled also by Auguste, the Judge's alter ego whose desire for Valentine we may assume the Judge will engineer.

The Judge places Valentine as the love object of his alter ego. It is this we view in the final sequences of the film. Up until this point in the film Auguste and Valentine have remained all but oblivious to each other, although he has looked with admiration at her blown up advertisement image which hangs over the streets of Geneva. Their encounter is nevertheless anticipated in the Judge's dream and intimated in the ending of the film. Here the Judge watches the television news footage of the notorious ferry disaster with which *Rouge* ends. The ferry disaster affords the Judge the opportunity to see Valentine and Auguste within the same frame and to realize the possibility of their future love for each other.

Here, significantly, the Judge is placed as spectator, viewing the visual narrative of trauma and survival from a distance. The meeting between Valentine and Auguste allows the Judge to see a potential drama of his own past re-enacted before his eyes. The dramatic links between his identity and that of Auguste allow the viewer to identify them with each other and to see the relation to Valentine as an act of wish-fulfilment. This seems itself a comment on the psychical investment in spectatorship, both televisual and cinematic, and on the means of visual media to repeat and reconstrue a single existence. The Judge depends on auditory and visual prostheses in order to apprehend an alternative history of his own life. Mass media bring him, ironically, as so often in Kieślowski's films, only what is already most intimate to him. The media through which the Judge views and listens to the outside world seem only to broadcast for him the images and sounds of his own inner life, as his memories coalesce with his fantasies.

v Cinematic Identities

Rouge is a film about endings, about the desire to look back upon one's life and reconsider its possibilities and alternative exits. This retrospective apprehension of parallel destinies, of possible choices, is central to the innovation of Kieślowski's filmmaking, to its unsettling appeal. In particular, retrospection, and the apprehension of the self in and through time, may impact on our understanding of identity. Kieślowski makes us rethink the representation of identity in cinema, revealing the ways in which the cinematic medium can work to uncover the temporal and psychical discontinuities of our perception of the self, its image and personal narratives.

The Judge's image in *Rouge* appears as a phantom presence, as his figure is seen through windows and in mirrors, in the reflecting surfaces and inner spaces of the house. As elsewhere in his film-making, Kieślowski calls the relation between virtual and actual into question. A further visual and psychological effect is created in the presentation of the Judge, allowing his youth to show through like a palimpsest, beneath the surface, beneath the skin. This depends on Kieślowski's choice of Jean-Louis Trintignant to play the part, relying it seems, as in his choice of Emmanuelle Riva in *Bleu*, on the viewer's knowledge of his face in its past animations (notably in *Ma Nuit chez Maud*). Already in *Rouge* the Judge's face is necessarily temporally sequenced for us. The Judge exists virtually as a discontinuous series of images in both spatial and temporal terms. This discontinuity and sequentiality is only enhanced in his dialogues with Valentine which necessarily in this house of memory encircle and resurrect his past. This is also resurrected, and redirected cinematically, as we have seen, in the presentation of Auguste's parallel destiny.

My question, then, is how Kieślowski's cinema intersects with, and re-orients, contemporary theories of identity. The notion of identity I am drawing on here is primarily psychoanalytic: specific insight can be found in the work of queer theorists who through their reading of both Freud and Lacan have worked to emphasize and expose the constructed nature of identity. The work of Judith Butler and Diana Fuss has recently, and variously, drawn attention to the differences, fissures and discontinuities which are inherent in a lived experience of selfhood. It is by virtue of this emphasis that their work proves illuminating in analysis of Kieślowski's cinema. His is a cinema of trauma and identification, of the imaginary investigation of other destinies such identification invokes. In exposing the differences within identity, Fuss and Butler return to this very question of identification and confirm its centrality as mechanism within the constitution of the psychic subject.

In her essay 'Imitation and Gender Insubordination', Butler contends that theories of identificatory mimetism or primary mimetism argue a strong position in favour of 'the non-self-identity of the psychic subject'.[15] In *Essentially Speaking*, Fuss makes use of a Lacanian understanding of identity as alienated and fictitious in order to argue that 'identity is rarely identical to itself but instead has multiple and sometimes contradictory meanings'.[16] She continues the trajectory of her thought in her more recent *Identification Papers* where she returns through Freud to argue that 'Identification inhabits, organizes, instantiates identity. It operates as a mark of self-difference, opening up a space for the self to relate to itself as a self, a self that is perpetually other.'[17] In their earlier work Butler and Fuss both use a notion of non-self-identity to radicalize thinking about gender and sexuality in fascinating and irrevocable ways. But it is the notion of alterity within identity which I want to think about further here, and which has more general implications for the ways in which we think selfhood and subjectivity (in the cinema). As she pursues her thought on identification, Fuss looks towards an understanding of the affective dimensions of non-self-identity and comes to anticipate the ways in which temporality and memory might always already intersect with this different, discontinuous image of the self.

It is the space where, in Fuss's terms, the self relates to itself as a self that is explored in Kieślowski's cinema. What Kieślowski emphasizes is indeed the space between the self and its image. This is figured literally in the distances and fissures between the selves of his protagonists and their mirrored, virtual reflections. This space is revealed further in the diegesis of both *La Double Vie de Véronique* and *Rouge* where the protagonist's alter ego is separated from him/her geographically in the first instance and temporally in the second. Mirroring, as we have seen, instantiates difference in Kieślowski's cinema. The self is always separate from itself. *Rouge* explores in particular the peculiar effect of self-difference tested in the context of memory, destiny and unlived lives.

Fuss identifies the memorial status of identification as psychic mechanism. She writes: 'Identification [...] invokes phantoms.' She explains this by showing how the subject incorporates the spectral remains of a lost love object in order to come into being. She confirms: 'To be open to an identification is to be open to a death encounter, open to the very possibility of communing with the dead.' Such an encounter seems the condition of selfhood, yet also its undoing. In this argument, identification leads us to set up a memorial to a lost other within the self, to entertain phantom presences in our selves. To quote Fuss again: 'These ghosts from the past can be neither casually summoned up nor wilfully conjured away. They are shadow others, the phantasmal relics of our complicated psychical histories.' In *Rouge* Kieślowski contends with the cinematic representation of such a complicated psychical history. Yet, if this film can function in a continuum with psychoanalytic theory, through the complexities of his use of the medium and our engagement with it, Kieślowski can lead us to image and imagine non-self-identity in different terms. Kieślowski imagines how the self may not merely set up a memorial to the other within itself, but also set up a memorial to the other the self might have been. This offers a more nuanced, more melancholy engagement with theories of identification. *Rouge* explores a complex intimation of the ways in which potential past selves as well as past lost objects inhabit and constitute the self. Kieślowski's protagonists mourn lost others, but also lost selves.

VI Melancholy Spectatorship

Identification is a vividly familiar concept in film theory, associated primarily with theories of spectatorship rather than with considerations of the construction of identity within particular films. Psychoanalytic theories of spectatorship have depended largely on a Lacanian model which posits distance and difference between the spectator and the ego ideal viewed on the screen. Metz, thinking about identification in the cinema, famously identifies the screen as mirror, yet reminds us that 'there is one thing and one thing only that is never reflected in it: the spectator's own body'.[18] This is a concept I have worked against in this study, looking at ways in which spectatorship itself is mirrored in

Kieślowski's cinema and at his search for recognition and uncanny familiarity in the experience of viewing. Through his visual narratives, where protagonists encounter their self, their image in the visual media, Kieślowski makes viewing itself a reckoning with identity, an experience of loss and discovery of selfhood.

This may lead us to wonder what might be at stake for the film critic in uncovering the Freudian bases of identification and its melancholic mechanism of incorporation and the othering of the self. Metz already reminds us that cinema is a memorial art form dependent on temporal *décalage*, offering us only ever an effigy of an object, infinitely desirable, never attainable. Barthes further recalls the link between photography and death, where the photographic image reminds us of the past status of what has been, the static image in stark contrast to the mortal figure it stills and represents. For Bazin, cinema as memorial art conserves not merely the still effigy of an object, but its movement and temporal existence. Kieślowski's cinema appears to draw attention to this melancholic dimension of the medium, as his protagonists are spectators mourning lost others and their lost selves. Viewing becomes not so much an act of identification with an ideal object as illusory recuperation of a lost object or lost self never possessed. Can we understand spectatorship in the cinema as retrospective as much as prospective, as bound with our desires for what we might have been? Does cinema allow us the illusion of viewing the phantom others whose loss we have denied in the constitution of our identities? Does cinema allow the glancing perception of other destinies, of virtual lives?

Kieślowski succeeds in his filmmaking in eliding the difference between virtual and actual in the image. His films have been veritably haunted by virtual reflections, images in mirrors, in crystal, in glass. His achievement in *Rouge* is to make us question the status not merely of the image but of the very identity of Auguste who may exist only ever as a virtual image of the Judge as he might have been. In unsettling our apprehension of his protagonists, Kieślowski encourages us to re-think our fictions of identity and of viewing. Identity may always be fissured and fractured by otherness; yet what may haunt and unsettle the self most insistently are the phantom images of the others she might have been. Cinema and its false identifications may allow us to disavow the loss of those others, yet its pleasures, as I think we see in the Judge's final expression in *Rouge*, remain only transient, illicit and illusory.

VII Filiations

In each discussion of Kieślowski's French cinema in this study, I have
stressed certain links between the individual films and work from the
French *Nouvelle Vague*. I have held off so far in discussion of *Rouge*: it
is in tracing a further pattern of filiation that this study will be brought
to a close. This necessitates firstly discussion of the very opening shots
of Kieślowski's last film.

Rouge begins with the sound of falling rain. This plays over the
opening credits and production details. The film's first signs are
auditory and ominous. The sound continues, enhanced by phantom
echoes of music over the first shots of the film where action begins
unexpectedly in England. We see a male hand pick up a receiver and
tap out a telephone number; beside the phone on the desk are a copy
of a novel by Aldous Huxley, a glass of whisky and a black and
white photo of a woman (Valentine). As the man waits for a reply the
camera moves slowly to the left, gradually picking up speed, passing
over the establishing details on the desk: a copy of *The Times*, a book
of first-class stamps. As our perspective moves more rapidly we become aware that the camera is following the length of the phone wire.
This passes over a map, the movements are more accelerated, slightly
jolting. The camera follows the wire into the darkness in the corner
of the room and then in a sudden bid for freedom, out into the underground reaches of its linear trajectory. The camera follows a vibrant
mass of red wires which disappear into a vortex in the centre of
the screen. The sense of speed and acceleration is increased still
further, and the image is rotated, offering a complete disruption of
conventional perception. Voices fade in and out of focus as we hear
the interfering conversations on the wires, their tone and timbre just
distorted by the speed of transmission. The scene plays on the viewer's
senses, working at a not quite conscious level.

The wires emerge in a series of cables which the camera follows
into the sea. As we see these shots we see drops of water which have
splashed onto the viewfinder. The camera moves very fast in a
forwards tracking shot and the image itself is accelerated so the viewer
is given the illusion of complete immersion. The shots have the
quality of cinematic dream narration: we are made aware of their
artifice and virtuosity, while questioning still their emotional effect.
The film plunges our viewpoint under the sea, as is only appropriate
in a narrative of drowning and survival. The water is turbid and

murky, even the fast-moving camera seems almost to lose its way. Is it here perhaps that we gain our first intimation in *Rouge* of the drowning which will be the film's culmination? While the camera never follows Valentine or Auguste in the decisive moments in the ferry disaster which determine their destiny and survival, nevertheless we will already have known, and seen, however unwittingly, a metonymic representation of that submersion and emergence. The camera has shifted again to follow the cables out of the water, onto the Continent, through a series of red hoops on the beach and into an eerily lit underground tunnel. The *mise-en-scène* here looks forward to the images of the bowling alley later in the film, and recalls again the interest in automatic movement which is witnessed throughout Kieślowski's cinema.

As the wires resonate in the tunnel, the voices they carry become more insistent to the viewer, though we can register the sound patterns only as moving, almost furious noise. The published screenplay of the film assures us that the wires carry conversations in different languages but that no words can be heard; as the wires cross out beyond the sea, 'le vacarme des conversations et des connexions va *crescendo*'.[19] The sense of this in the context of a European trilogy is clear. *Rouge* starts in interconnection; it is a film which alludes continually to its own allusive and interconnected status. This only confirms its resonance as a film of culmination and reckoning where threads are drawn together.

The automatism of the moving viewpoint itself culminates in a series of near abstract rotating images. The screen is dominated by flashing lights in kaleidoscope effect as the viewer perceives '[les] lumières clignotantes d'une centrale'. The call then reaches its destination as the titles break over the screen. A red light flashes and the image is now dominated by the pulse of the engaged signal. This seems almost painful as it blocks communication between Michel and Valentine, placing the film under a sign of failure and alarm. The camera moves in closer to the red light so its warning colour dominates the screen (as it will so many times elsewhere in the film).[20] We cut back to Michel's apartment where we see him put down the receiver.

Rouge is a film cross-cut by telephone conversations which establish aural and affective links and breaks between its central protagonists. The filmmaker (and viewer) finds his/her role reflected in the position of the Judge who sits at the nexus of this series of threads, eavesdropping on the conversations around him, living vicariously, impassively as he bears silent (and illegal) witness to the lives of his neighbours. The threads of the phone wires, of the interconnected conversations, are rendered also in Kieślowski's cinema threads of destiny, threads of parallel, unconscious and controlled existences. Filiation becomes a central motif as *Rouge* unwinds.

One pattern of filiation I want to stress is crucially cinematic. In opening his film in communication, and imitating in illusory manner the trajectory of the telephone wires, Kieślowski alludes liberally to Truffaut and a similar device used humorously in *Baisers volés*, the third in the sequence of Antoine Doinel films. Here the all but adult Doinel sends a telegram to break off his affair with the older Fabienne. We hear him read the letter in voice-over as he walks to a collection box labelled 'Pneumatiques'. The camera offers us a close-up image of the envelope and its address as it is posted and then collected by a postal worker. The envelope is stamped twice and then deposited in a canister to be sent rapidly through Paris to its destination. Truffaut's camera follows the path of the telegram pipe, first filming it from the exterior (as imitated in *Rouge*) and then suddenly seizing an optical omniscience as the viewpoint dives into the underground passages of Paris, claiming the power to view the body of the city laparo-scopically. The camera pauses momentarily at a series of blue and white street signs which codify this underground, fantasy city as clearly as their counterparts work above. This adds humorous effect as we follow the precipitate course of the telegram, hearing its move-ment in the whirr and whistle of the pipes. While the image is rendered as literal as peculiarly possible, it also seems to imitate the paranoid anticipation of Doinel's imagination as the course of the telegram and its outcome become unavoidable. The telegram canister arrives at its destination, is unpacked, and is opened by Fabienne's elegant hands.

A telegram which signals the end of an affair seems an apt point of return in *Rouge*: the missive itself seems of significance. Yet more than this it is the form as much as the content of Kieślowski's tribute to Truffaut which seems important. Truffaut more than any of the directors of the *Nouvelle Vague* may be seen by his own theoretical designation, his youthful journalism and first-person filmmaking as a French *auteur* and as passionate cinephile. *Baisers volés* opens with an ironic tribute to the *cinémathèque* in Paris and to Henri Langlois. Placing this film as palimpsest in the inception of *Rouge*, Kieślowski cannot fail to attempt to situate his cinema in a French tradition. Here it is not so much French national identity or even society or terrain which counts (*Rouge* is set in Geneva and strives for the anodyne Pan-European sensibility some have found in *Bleu*): it is French Cinema and its visual and narrative heritage which Kieślowski recalls and celebrates. This is a part of his cinema's memorial and commemorative appeal; it also defines its melancholy and its specific intimation of the death and end of *auteur* cinema as associated with art-house values and intellectual, even metaphysical themes.

In the form of his filmmaking Truffaut also offers Kieślowski a telling point of reference in terms of patterns of filiation and inter-connection. Truffaut has amply illustrated the imbrication of cinema, memory and the re-projection of past lives. His Antoine Doinel series is a touchstone in a tradition of autobiographical cinema in France.

Of particular relevance to Kieślowski's trilogy as a whole is the last Antoine Doinel film, *L'Amour en fuite* (1979). There are numerous echoes of this film in the trilogy. Most notable perhaps are the debts to the scene of the divorce of Antoine and Christine, which is central to the action of *L'Amour en fuite*. In Truffaut's divorce scene, Antoine looks briefly out of the window to see a wedding party in the street below. The sudden view seems an image counterpointed with the divorce scene and an objective correlative of Antoine's state of mind as divorce triggers brief nostalgia for his marriage. As we have seen in discussion of *Blanc*, the white wedding is more literally a memory image, fantasy and point of longing in Kieślowski's trilogy. In broader terms, Truffaut's means of evoking memory images and psychical reality offers its own inspiration to Kieślowski. In *L'Amour en fuite*, Truffaut playfully uses clips from earlier episodes in the Antoine Doinel series, as well as other confected memory images, to offer a reflection on memory which is self-consciously cinematic.[21] This liberal intercutting of shots and time frames serves both to periodize Truffaut's own filmmaking and to offer a seductive illusion of continuity and historical depth to the filmic life history of Antoine Doinel. Truffaut here actualizes a link between the cinematic image and the memory image in ways which anticipate Kieślowski's later interest in temporal sequence in cinema and in the representation of mental and mnemonic function.

Kieślowski's trilogy is by no means so directly representational, yet it takes up Truffaut's concerns with using cinema to explore destiny (in Truffaut's case personal, in Kieślowski's collective). In alluding to *Baisers volés* in *Rouge*, and the Antoine Doinel series more generally in the trilogy, Kieślowski takes an overtly cinematic representation of communication, a flashy demonstration of the power of the moving image, and of the moving images it may take as its subject, and repeats it as moving tribute in his last film. Communication between levels of cinematic past, the resurrection of virtual images, of filmed lives is evidently his subject in the trilogy.

VIII   Cinema, Death and the Still Image

One of the most lasting images Truffaut has left narrative cinema is the stilled picture of Antoine Doinel at the end of *Les Quatre Cents Coups*. The child Léaud, whose pose and stillness have been frequently copied, is frozen in a moment of great emotion, yet without unambiguous meaning. Truffaut stops at the end of his film with no resolution, only stasis and confrontation. This ending serves to draw the medium itself into question, drawing attention to its illusion of motion, generated from the projection of stilled images. It is as if Antoine catches the viewer looking at him in these last few moments, as if this recognition disrupts any suspension of disbelief in the film, stills its image and allows the camera, in its voyeuristic, predatory way, now to close in on his face as a stilled artefact as we watch it staring, artificially frozen. There is an illusion of control over this final image, yet this control comes with a realization of the voyeurism inherent in spectatorship. Antoine, like the viewer, is caught like a suspect imprisoned in the image which avows now its own photographic status.

In *Rouge*, Kieślowski pursues Truffaut's deconstruction of movement and stasis in the cinematic image. This is achieved most directly in the viewing scenario at the end of the film where the Judge watches the news footage of Valentine's survival. Here Kieślowski negotiates a series of still and moving images, in a manner which in part brings into question the realism of his news footage reconstruction. The Judge's first realization of the accident comes as he collects his newspaper in the morning and sees a black and white photograph of the ferry on its side in the sea. Indoors he urgently switches on his television; the black and white photograph is swiftly replaced by similar news footage of the disaster, a moving image, a long shot filmed in colour in appropriately early morning light. We are shown that the images are shot from a helicopter which circles round the scene of the disaster, offering it as a panoramic view. The series of shots is intercut with images of the Judge, as he watches this narrative of a disaster of his imagination. We see images of the rescue, of anonymous bodies hauled to freedom. These are shot with a spotlight and surrounding darkness. The news footage is composed of several layers of temporal sequence as it offers an edited visual trace of the disaster and its aftermath. The voice over then cuts to mention of survivors and we see the photographers and news cameramen rushing towards the centre of the frame, its point of focus and taut expectation. The next shots are signalled as photographic images, as fixed trace of the momentous event. This is reflected in the visual treatment of the scene of survival. Gradually we see the escaped figures come forward. The first is Julie, recognizable from *Bleu*, repeating her own earlier survival of trauma. As Kieślowski begins this seeming litany of commemoration, remembering the first two parts of the trilogy in the final images of the third, he allows the camera to linger on Julie and allows the image, for a moment, to be artificially stilled. This seems to serve several purposes.

Time seems aptly drawn out as the film privileges duration over logical temporal sequence. The dramatic importance of the moment draws the image to a halt, lets its trace be indelibly marked on the mind. This must be the mind of the viewer in the film and the viewer of the film. Embedding the Judge as spectator here, Kieślowski invests these shots with tremendous emotional charge as, on a first-time viewing, we are encouraged to share Kern's fear and hope that Valentine will survive. The image represents in this sense the very numbing of Kern's mind as he awaits Valentine's apotheosis. Equally the stilling of the image might work to reflect on the specificity of the medium—television—in which the Judge hopes to view Valentine's survival. Kieślowski explores the ways in which freeze frame and repetition have become a feature of television viewing through the capacity of video as medium. In this sense, this form of spectatorship offers the illusory control over the image which the Judge seeks. Literally, or in his mind's eye, the Judge keeps and stills the survivors in his frame of vision. For the viewer, more practically, it seems that the image lingers to ensure that we capture its full impact and meaning.

The device is repeated to honour each of the other survivors, with the exception of the unknown British barman, Stephen Killian, whose presence goes unexplained in the trilogy. Stilled in close-up we see the recognizable faces of Karol, Dominique, Olivier, Auguste and finally Valentine. In this last image, which is treated with the most liberal disregard for temporal convention as it stays long moments on the screen, Kieślowski achieves a further effect of uncanny doubling. The image is constructed to appear natural and entirely contingent. Valentine, like the other survivors, is wrapped in a grey blanket. Her hair is wet, her face pale and haunted. She is protectively close to Auguste, but turns away from him for a moment so that her face is silhouetted, first against a crowd of cameramen, and then, as one of the rescue workers passes behind her, against the strident red of his waterproof garments. This image in profile, with its red background, is captured as a still image for the Judge and for the viewer. As it is seen first, Auguste is visible beside Valentine. Gradually the camera moves to draw her face alone into focus and it is instantly obvious that the image we view here is a near copy (or a source?) of the advertising shot of Valentine, with which Auguste has been fascinated and which has hung over Geneva for the second half of the film. It has been seen, indeed, dismantled in pouring rain in the shots which immediately precede the disaster scene.

This uncanny doubling allows the possibility that the advertising image stands as illusory flashforward to the moment of survival at the end of *Rouge* (in a device reminiscent of *Blanc*). Kieślowski again seems to disrupt temporal sequence where the moment of survival is seen to be known always already in the advertising image which has apparently preceded it. This familiarity seems only to enhance the emotional charge attached to the image of survival.

Comparison of the two images, and their construction, also reveals a different thread in Valentine's destiny and a further parallel narrative which intersects with her encounter with the Judge. In some senses the Judge has constructed Valentine's destiny in bringing her to the ferry disaster as he persuades her to go by boat, and disregards the storm brewing over Europe, leading her inexorably to encounter Auguste, his alter ego. Yet he is not alone in choreographing Valentine's life. She is also literally directed by Jacques, the photographer who organizes the shoot in which the advertising image is taken. In this scene (which is markedly different in the screenplay and the completed film) the photographer painstakingly constructs the image we later see. He directs Valentine to take out her gum, to put her grey sweater about her shoulders, and he continues: 'Sois triste. Plus triste. Pense à quelque chose de terrible. Voilà.' She achieves his vision, as it were, as the film constructs a pre-view of survival. The photographer's instructions are realistic in constructing the image. Kieślowski draws attention to the ways in which images themselves are artificially produced, to the ways in which the material world is constructed rather than captured by the camera. Jacques is responsible for the construction of Valentine's image. Aptly, like the Judge, he has some romantic interest in her, attempting to kiss her in a later scene and inviting her to go bowling. The Judge recognizes indeed that Jacques takes Valentine to the same bowling rink on the same evening as Auguste takes Karin. Lightly Kieślowski seems to suggest that there may be an alternative destiny for Valentine diverging partly from Kern's directive plan.

Jacques and the Judge are both, then, viewers of Valentine who recognize and are moved by the image of her face in distress. The film's spectator may be led to question the way in which this doubling of the Judge's viewing position impacts on our understanding of the film. Julia Dobson in a stringent and brilliant commentary on the film argues:

> The revelation of the artificial construction of the image, and our recognition of its previous role, call into question the authenticity of both Valentine's sad expression and of the function of the cinematic image before us. Our subsequent reflection both on the manipulation of the image and the parallel manipulation of our positions as spectator-consumer obliges us to question whether the discourses of financial and emotional investment can be mutually accommodated.[22]

Her scepticism seems important, yet I find it significant too that in the film's teleology (if we allow temporal sequence priority once more) it is the contingent image which supersedes the advertising shot. I would argue that Kieślowski overrides the glossy image with the final intimation of fear and survival.

In the second occurrence of the repeated image, Kieślowski seems to contend further with questions of life, death and survival, all of which are intimately bound up with the photographic medium (as we have seen in reference to Metz, Barthes and Bazin above). Here again the potential of Kieślowski's cinema as cinema of trauma is brought to the fore. The Judge has already lost his first female love and object of desire in an accident. He tells Valentine of the way this woman betrayed him with another man: 'Hugo Holbling... c'était son nom... pouvait lui donner ce qu'elle voulait. Ils sont partis. Je les ai suivis, j'ai traversé la France, la Manche, j'ai été en Ecosse, et encore plus loin... J'ai été humilié. Jusqu'au jour où elle est morte, dans un accident.'[23] The crossing of the Channel is repeated by Auguste (and Valentine). The fate of the blonde woman seems to be repeated in the death of

Karin who we surmise is the victim, with her new lover, of the yachting accident which happens in the tempest of the ferry disaster. Yet the Judge risks also repeating his own loss in the feared death of Valentine: he cannot guarantee that she will survive the disaster to supplant and disavow the loss of the previously missed object of desire. We may question whether the Judge returns in his mind to the site of his trauma, compulsively seeking its virtual repetition. Such compulsion would certainly be legitimate in the light of Freud's work and later studies of post-traumatic stress disorder (as discussed in Chapter 2). The returns and repetitions of Kieślowski's filmmaking take on in this light a more pathological and determined status. But perhaps the Judge merely returns to a scenario from the past to live it out and live it through differently. The film seems to ask whether past trauma can be neutralized in present survival. Can the risk of the loss of Valentine and the realization of her survival recuperate the years of solipsism the Judge appears to have spent in his house? Is the repetition of love and loss mere chance in his life? Or a device to create order and recognition in viewing? These questions remain effectively unanswered for the viewer yet inhere in her experience of viewing the last memorial image of *Rouge*.

This compulsion to repeat seems manifested too in Kieślowski's filmmaking. Trauma, which is so frequently his subject, seems also to determine the formal structure of his films and their compulsive, repetitive interlayering of reference. This is of course willed on the filmmaker's part, yet willingly obsessional. The images of his films are mnemonic in several senses. They work to represent the past, present and future memory traces of his chosen protagonists and of their temporal, subjective filtering of reality. Yet they function too both to repeat and re-present the images not only of Kieślowski's own films, but of the national cinema in which he seeks to find his place. In the parting shot of *Rouge*, Kieślowski represents the Judge's past and future desires, the stilled image which will have served as the focal point in the trial of his identity the film becomes. This focal point is, nevertheless, vertiginous. In the final image are reflected the earlier image in *Rouge*, photographic images in *La Double Vie de Véronique* and the stilled image in *Les Quatre Cents Coups* which has been a source in this discussion. In these patterns of reflection, the relation between internal and external, same and different is rendered entirely indeterminate.

In *La Double Vie de Véronique* the relation between stilled and moving images has been, as we have seen, linked to questions of life, death, survival and commemoration. The photographic image itself is a major subject of the film, as I have argued. This is exploited specifically in the recognition scene where Véronique, studying her own holiday pictures at Alexandre's insistence, realizes that she has an uncanny double (as she has sensed intuitively throughout the film). The still photograph she sees, with the image of Weronika, is one of a series of images. Literally it is shown to be one of a series of holiday pictures. On a self-reflexive level it works to reveal the very raw material, the set of stilled images out of which film is generated. The image of Weronika recalls her presence for us and commemorates her prior existence in the temporal sequence of the film. It becomes her *memento mori*. The still photograph commemorates also the scene of interference between the existences of Weronika and Véronique. The still image recalls images in motion, reminding us of the uncanny capacity of film to create an illusion of movement out of stasis, an illusion of life out of death.

The image of Valentine at the end of *Rouge*, stilled in silence for some moments before the credits roll, carries with it the fear of death in the stasis of the image and in the disaster of the film's narrative. The film appears to hesitate between commemoration and survival. Cinema is explored as medium which allows the generation of movement from stasis, of virtual existences extending beyond the bounds of temporal and material reality.

Notes to Chapter 4

1. Kieślowski says in interview: 'Ce que j'ai l'intention de faire maintenant? Je peux prendre une chaise, un paquet de cigarettes, un café, et me mettre à lire. Il y a tant de livres que je n'ai pas eu le temps de lire, et tant d'autres que je voudrais relire une quatrième et une soixante-quatorzième fois. Cela suffit jusqu'à la fin d'une vie.' 'Ma vie est tout ce que je possède', *Positif* 423 (May 1996), 75–6, 76.
2. I am grateful to Mick Thurston for first drawing this to my attention.
3. Agnès Peck, '*Trois Couleurs Bleu/Blanc/Rouge*: Une trilogie européenne', in *Krzysztof Kieślowski*, ed. Michel Estève (Paris, 1994),147–62, 159, 160.
4. Kehr, 'To Save the World', 18, 18, 20.
5. Philip Kemp, '*Trois Couleurs: Rouge*', *Sight and Sound* 4/11 (Nov. 1994), 54–5, 55, 55.
6. Geoff Andrew makes a very different reading of the ending of *Rouge*, one which does not fit with the latent pessimism of my account but is in itself persuasive and appealing. He writes: 'Seeing the protagonists of *Blue* and *White* take their place as survivors alongside those of *Red*, we are not only given hope regarding their (hitherto ambiguous) futures, but we may somehow feel that we the

audience have been rewarded by Kieślowski for taking a sympathetic interest in their fates' (*The 'Three Colours' Trilogy*, 61).

7. Stephen Pizzello, 'Piotr Sobociński: *Red*', *American Cinematographer* 76/6 (June 1995), 68–74, 71.

8. Stok (ed.), *Kieślowski on Kieślowski*, 220.

9. Andrew cites Kieślowski saying *Rouge* is his most personal film.

10. Kieślowski, *Trois Couleurs* III, 19, 19.

11. Amiel comments all the more affirmatively: 'Dans *La Double Vie de Véronique* comme dans *Rouge*, c'est le retour au père qui permet la survie, c'est la mémoire et le repli qui assurent un présent chaotique, la survie, la contraction du temps, l'équilibre de ses oscillations' (*Kieślowski*, 16).

12. Slavoj Žižek, 'No Sexual Relationship', in *Gaze and Voice as Love Objects*, ed. R. Saleci and S. Žižek (Durham, NC, and London, 1996), 208–49, 238.

13. Kieślowski, *Trois Couleurs* III, 78, 78, 78, 78.

14. Stok (ed.), *Kieślowski on Kieślowski*, 6, 218, 218, 218.

15. Judith Butler, 'Imitation and Gender Insubordination', in *Inside/Out*, ed. Diana Fuss (London, 1991), 13–31, 26.

16. Diana Fuss, *Essentially Speaking: Feminism, Nature and Difference* (London, 1989), 98.

17. Diana Fuss, *Identification Papers* (London, 1995), 2, 1, 1, 2.

18. Metz, *Psychoanalysis and Cinema*, 45.

19. Kieślowski, *Trois Couleurs* III, 6, 6.

20. This red screen is already uncannily pre-viewed in *La Double Vie de Véronique* when Véronique listens to Alexandre's recording of the Van der Budenmayer (or Preisner) music Weronika sang in her dying performance. The image appears as an unconscious memory trace, triggered, it seems, by the music. The red screen looks forward to *Rouge* but is always already blotted by an anamorphic image, a pale distorted face in the corner of our field of vision, which appears as a memory or reminder of death.

21. The trilogy may also be seen to be indebted to the self-reflexivity of Truffaut's filmmaking in its repetition of the thematics of voyeurism, proximity and distance as explored in *Antoine et Colette* (1962). For further discussion of links between Kieślowski and Truffaut, see Insdorf, *Double Lives, Second Chances*, 5.

22. Julia Dobson, 'Nationality, authenticity, reflexivity: Kieślowski's *Three Colours: Blue* (1993), *White* (1993) and *Red* (1994)', in *French Cinema in the 1990s: Continuity and Difference*, ed. Phil Powrie (Oxford, 1999), 234–45.

23. Kieślowski, *Trois Couleurs* III, 99.

CONCLUSION

Home Movies

In Krzysztof Wierzbicki's documentary, *Krzysztof Kieślowski: I'm So So* (1996), Kieślowski indicates that when he is filming abroad, he always wants to go home. Speaking about his memories, he says he recalls little of his earliest childhood. There is little basis for his memories, he suggests, since his family moved all the time. In interview with Danusia Stok, he explains further:

My father had tuberculosis and for twelve years after the Second World War he was dying of it. He'd go to sanatoria and since we wanted to be near him—my mum, that is, and the two of us, me and my sister—we'd follow him. He'd be in a sanatorium and my mum would work in an office in the same town. He'd go to another sanatorium and we'd move to another town.[1]

In the photographs which accompany Stok's text, an anxious infant Kieślowski can be seen sheltered by his mother in a hood and cape. In another image, slightly older, he is pictured with his mother and his sister at a sanatorium. These images of a restless and melancholy childhood, their narrative of displacement and longing, work as a phantom image, a lost memory trace in the cinema of survival and denial Kieślowski develops at home and abroad.

I have argued here that Kieślowski's French cinema draws on a complex dialectics of sameness and difference. Familiarity is fostered in attempts to replicate, repeat, even remember the images and emotions of his earlier Polish cinema. Yet these images are themselves doubled (as in *La Double Vie de Véronique*) by images drawn from a very different cinematic repertoire, paying homage to the national cinema in whose confines Kieślowski's cinema finds its final location. Throughout his cinema, indeed, Kieślowski works both to correlate and to confuse the memory image and the cinematic image to such an extent that any divisions between actual and virtual, subjective and objective, personal and public are denied. His films make up a cinema of doubling and proliferation; hence the importance of the three major theoretical strands in this discussion.

Reading Kieślowski through Deleuze has allowed specific focus on the historical and aesthetic context of Kieślowski's cinema (within Deleuze's periodization of the history and theory of film). Such a framework has afforded some of the links established between Kieślowski and French directors, in particular Resnais, Rohmer and Godard. Evidently much work is still to be done both on the possibilities of cinema post the time-image, and more specifically on the influence Kieślowski will have had on the future development of French national cinema. Such a prospective survey, necessarily outside the bounds of the present study, might again open new ways of thinking about hybridity in film and about how national cinemas are always already open to infiltration and identificatory mechanisms whereby what is alien is absorbed, repeated and reproduced.

Deleuze's thinking on the memorial and fantasmatic potential of cinema as art form has been supplemented in this study with further reference to other accounts of memory malfunction and trauma which are more psychoanalytic in bias. This second theoretical strand has allowed me to draw attention to the ways in which Kieślowski's cinema arguably offers its own intervention in thinking about trauma and survival, some of the most charged human and theoretical issues of the 1990s. Here again a dialectics of sameness and difference returns where Kieślowski's cinema may be seen to explore the temporal disruption and the imperfect repetitions of traumatic re-enactment. Psychic malfunction becomes a means to cinematic re-invention, yet the cinema of trauma also becomes the means to meditating on possibilities of recovery and survival in denial. By no means is Kieślowski's cinema prescriptive in its representations or in the responses it generates. Instead it seeks to bring the viewer to a point of recognizing failed vision and failure to understand, courting forbearance, perhaps, and at most patience and compassion.

Contrary to many critics, I maintain that Kieślowski's cinema is profoundly pessimistic, if tender and elegiac. He offers an image of existence always already fissured by loss, longing and incompletion. This accounts for the ways in which work by queer theorists who have privileged the constructed, incomplete and non-self-identical status of identity, has emerged as the third major theoretical strand in this study. Despite its seeming return to conventional narratives of sexual difference and heterosexual love, Kieślowski's cinema probes the losses and illusions of such histories, their imperfect repetition of the family romance, their dependence on power play, distance and manipulation.

Where my readings have privileged the human material, the mental images, dramas and identity tests of his protagonists, I have sought also to emphasize throughout the self-reflexive dimensions of Kieślowski's filmmaking, his interest in and dependence on fictions of viewing, framing and representation. Individual desires and emotions are caught in the frame of Kieślowski's filmmaking, where betrayal and the very risks of representation are all too frequently his subject. Further, Kieślowski illustrates the imbrication of human existence, the visual media and their structures of voyeurism, spectacle and spectatorial distance. In recognizing this, the viewer too is drawn to find her own spectatorial activity mirrored in the frame, in a Proustian reflection on the subjectivity of reception.

Kieślowski's French cinema is a cinema of willed exile, a cinema at one remove. In exploring survival, these films privilege futurity and forgetting in the face of the irredeemable loss of the past. Yet the transition in mood and emotion from *Bleu* to *Rouge* is not insignificant. The last film depends ultimately on the avowal of the painful pleasures of cinema as commemorative medium in which to re-view, in illusory and moving forms, lost selves, lost others and lost memories of the past. The illicit pleasure of this cinema lies in its nostalgia, in the indiscernibility of virtual and actual images which it illustrates so compulsively. The indiscernibility is, contrary to Deleuze, revealed as a source of psychic disturbance and delusion. Kieślowski's French cinema is both prospective and retrospective. In its return to spaces where doubling holds pleasure in denial, it achieves the subversion of a normative teleology of symbolization opening cinema as space and place of melancholic pleasure, and of psychosis. For Kieślowski uncanny familiarity is sought despite distance and difference. While he makes films abroad, he stays resolutely at home.

Note to Concluding Remarks

1. Stok (ed.), *Kieślowski on Kieślowski*, 2–5. See also Insdorf, *Double Lives, Second Chances*, 6–7, for a further account of Kieślowski's childhood.

FILMOGRAPHY

1966
Tramwaj (The Tram)
Director: Krzysztof Kieślowski
Screenplay: Krzysztof Kieślowski
Cinematography: Zdzisław Kaczmarek
Production Company: Łódź Film School
Short Feature   35 mm black and white   5 mins 45 secs

Urząd (The Office)
Director: Krzysztof Kieślowski
Screenplay: Krzysztof Kieślowski
Cinematography: Lechosław Trzęsowski
Production Company: Łódź Film School
Documentary   35 mm black and white   6 mins

1967
Koncert Życzeń (Concert of Requests)
Director: Krzysztof Kieślowski
Screenplay: Krzysztof Kieślowski
Cinematography: Lechosław Trzęsowski
Editor: Janina Grosicka
Production Company: Łódź Film School
Feature   35 mm black and white   17 mins

1968
Zdjęcie (The Photograph)
Director: Krzysztof Kieślowski
Cinematography: Marek Jóźwiak
Editor: Niusia Ciucka
Production Company: Polish Television
Documentary   16 mm black and white   32 mins

1969
Z Miasta Łodzi (From the City of Łódź)
Director: Krzysztof Kieślowski
Cinematography: Januscz Kreczmański, Piotr Kwiatkowski, Stanisław Niedbalski
Editors: Elżbieta Kurkowska, Lidia Zonn
Sound: Krystyna Pohorecka
Production Company: WFD
Documentary   35 mm black and white   17 mins 21 secs

1970
Byłem Żolnierzem (I Was a Soldier)
Director: Krzysztof Kieślowski
Screenplay: Krzysztof Kieślowski, Ryszard Zgórecki
Cinematography: Stanisław Niedbalski
Production Company: Czołówka
Documentary   35 mm black and white   16 mins

Fabryka (Factory)
Director: Krzysztof Kieślowski
Cinematography: Stanisław Niedbalski, Jacek Tworek
Editor: Maria Leszczyńska
Sound: Małgorzata Jaworska
Production Company: WFD
Documentary   35 mm black and white   17 mins 14 secs

1971
Przed Rajdem (Before the Rally)
Director: Krzysztof Kieślowski
Cinematography: Piotr Kwiatowski, Jacek Petrycki
Editor: Lidia Zonn
Sound: Małgorzata Jaworska
Production Company: WFD
Documentary   35 mm black and white/colour   15 mins 9 secs

1972
Refren (Refrain)
Director: Krzysztof Kieślowski
Cinematography: Witold Stok
Editor: Maryla Czołnik
Sound: Małgorzata Jaworska, Michał Żarnecki
Production Company: WFD
Documentary   35 mm black and white   10 mins 19 secs

Między Wrocławiem a Zieloną Górą (Between Wroclaw and Zielona Gora)
Director: Krzysztof Kieślowski
Cinematography: Jacek Petrycki
Editor: Lidia Zonn
Sound: Andrzej Bohdanowicz
Production Company: WFD, commissioned by Lubin Copper Mine
Commissioned film   35 mm colour   10 mins 35 secs

Podstawy BHP w Kopalnii Miedzi (The Principles of Safety and Hygiene in a Copper Mine)
Director: Krzysztof Kieślowski
Cinematography: Jacek Petrycki
Editor: Lidia Zonn
Sound: Andrzej Bohdanowicz
Production Company: WFD, commissioned by Lubin Copper Mine
Commissioned film   35 mm colour   20 mins 52 secs

Robotnicy '71: Nic o nas bez nas (Workers '71: Nothing about us without us)
Director: Krzysztof Kieślowski
Cinematography: Jacek Petrycki
Editor: Lidia Zonn
Sound: Andrzej Bohdanowicz
Production Company: WFD
Documentary   16 mm black and white   46 mins 39 secs

1973
Murarz (Bricklayer)
Director: Krzysztof Kieślowski
Cinematography: Witold Stok
Editor: Lidia Zonn
Sound: Małgorzata Jaworska
Production Company: WFD
Documentary   35 mm colour   17 mins 39 secs

Przejście Podziemne (Pedestrian Subway)
Director: Krzysztof Kieślowski
Screenplay: Ireneusz Iredyński, Krzysztof Kieślowski
Cinematography: Sławomir Idziak
Sound: Małgorzata Jaworska
Production Company: Polish Television
TV drama   35 mm black and white   30 mins

1974

Prześwietlenie (X-Ray)
Director: Krzysztof Kieślowski
Cinematography: Jacek Petrycki
Editor: Lidia Zonn
Sound: Michał Żarnecki
Documentary   35 mm colour   13 mins

Pierwsza Miłość (First Love)
Director: Krzysztof Kieślowski
Cinematography: Jacek Petrycki
Editor: Lidia Zonn
Sound: Małgorzata Jaworska, Michał Żarnecki
Production Company: Polish Television
TV documentary   16 mm colour   30 mins

1975

Życiorys (Curriculum vitae)
Director: Krzysztof Kieślowski
Screenplay: Janusz Fastyn, Krzysztof Kieślowski
Cinematography: Jacek Petrycki, Tadeusz Rusinek
Editor: Lidia Zonn
Sound: Spaś Christow
Production Company: WFD
Drama documentary   35 mm black and white   45 mins 10 secs

Personel (Personnel)
Director: Krzysztof Kieślowski
Screenplay: Krzysztof Kieślowski
Cinematography: Witold Stok
Editor: Lidia Zonn
Production Company: Polish Television and Tor Production
Cast: Juliusz Machulski (*Romek*)
TV drama   16 mm colour   72 mins

1976

Szpital (Hospital)
Director: Krzysztof Kieślowski
Cinematography: Jacek Petrycki
Editor: Lidia Zonn
Sound: Michał Żarnecki
Production Company: WFD
Documentary   35 mm black and white   21 mins 4 secs

Blizna (The Scar)
Director: Krzysztof Kieślowski
Screenplay: Krzysztof Kieślowski, based on a story by Romuald Karaś
Cinematography: Sławomir Idziak
Editor: Krystyna Górnicka
Sound: Michał Żarnecki
Production Company: Tor Production
Cast: Franciszek Pieczka (*Bednarz*)
Feature   35 mm colour   104 mins

Spokój (The Calm)
Director: Krzysztof Kieślowski
Screenplay: Krzysztof Kieślowski, based on a story by Lech Borski
Cinematography: Jacek Petrycki
Editor: Maryla Szymańska
Sound: Wiesław Jurgała
Production Company: Polish Television
Cast: Jerzy Stuhr (*Antek Gralak*)
TV drama   16 mm colour   44 mins

1977
Z Punktu Widzenia Nocnego Portiera (From a Night Porter's Point of View)
Director: Krzysztof Kieślowski
Cinematography: Witold Stok
Editor: Lidia Zonn
Sound: Wiesława Dembinska, Michał Żarnecki
Production Company: WFD
Documentary   35 mm colour   16 mins 52 secs

Nie wiem (I Don't Know)
Director: Krzysztof Kieślowski
Cinematography: Jacek Petrycki
Editor: Lidia Zonn
Sound: Michał Żarnecki
Production Company: WFD
Documentary   35 mm black and white   46 mins 27 secs

1978
Siedem Kobiet w Różnym Wieku (Seven Women of Different Ages)
Director: Krzysztof Kieślowski
Cinematography: Witold Stok
Editors: Alina Siemińska, Lidia Zonn

Sound: Michał Żarnecki
Production Company: WFD
Documentary   35 mm black and white   16 mins

1979
Amator (Camera Buff)
Director: Krzysztof Kieślowski
Screenplay: Krzysztof Kieślowski
Cinematography: Jacek Petrycki
Editor: Halina Nawrocka
Sound: Michał Żarnecki
Production Company: Tor
Cast: Jerzy Stuhr (*Filip Mosz*), Małgorzata Ząbkowska (*Irka Mosz*), Ewa Pokas (*Anna Włodarczyk*), Stefan Czyżewski (*Manager*), Jerzy Nowak (*Osuch*), Tadeusz Bradecki (*Witek*), Marek Litewka (*Piotrek Krawczyk*), Bogusław Sobczuk (*Television editor*), Krzysztof Zanussi (*himself*)
Feature   35 mm colour   112 mins

1980
Dworzec (Station)
Director: Krzysztof Kieślowski
Cinematography: Witold Stok
Editor: Lidia Zonn
Sound: Michał Żarnecki
Production Company: WFD
Documentary   35 mm black and white   13 mins 23 secs

Gadające Głowy (Talking Heads)
Director: Krzysztof Kieślowski
Cinematography: Jacek Petrycki, Piotr Kwiatkowski
Editor: Alina Siemińska
Sound: Michał Żarnecki
Production Company: WFD
Documentary   35 mm black and white   15 mins 32 secs

1981
Przypadek (Blind Chance)
Director: Krzysztof Kieślowski
Screenplay: Krzysztof Kieślowski
Cinematography: Krzysztof Pakulski
Editor: Elżbieta Kurkowska
Sound: Michał Żarnecki

Production Company: Tor
Cast: Bogusław Linda (*Witek*), Tadeusz Łomnicki (*Werner*), Bogusława Pawełec (*Czuszka*), Zbigniew Zapasiewicz (*Adam*), Jacek Borkowski (*Marek*), Adam Ferency (*Priest*), Jacek Sas-Uchrynowski (*Daniel*), Marzena Trybała (*Werka*), Irena Burska (*Aunt*), Monika Goździk (*Olga*), Zbigniew Hübner (*Principal*)
Feature 35 mm colour 122 mins

Krótki Dzień Pracy (Short Working Day)
Director: Krzysztof Kieślowski
Screenplay: Hanna Krall, Krzysztof Kieślowski
Cinematography: Krzysztof Pakulski
Editor: Elżbieta Kurkowska
Sound: Michał Żarnecki
Production Company: Polish Television
Cast: Wacław Ulewicz (*Party Secretary*)
Feature 35 mm colour 79 mins 33 secs

1984
Bez Końca (No End)
Director: Krzysztof Kieślowski
Screenplay: Krzysztof Kieślowski, Krzysztof Piesiewicz
Cinematography: Jacek Petrycki
Editor: Krystyna Rutkowska
Sound: Michał Żarnecki
Music: Zbigniew Preisner
Production Company: Tor
Cast: Grażyna Szapołowska (*Urszula Zyro*), Maria Pakulnis (*Joanna*), Aleksander Bardini (*Labrador*), Jerzy Radziwiłłowicz (*Antoni Zyro*), Artur Barciś (*Dariusz*), Michał Bajor (*Apprentice lawyer*), Marek Kondrat (*Tomek*), Tadeusz Bradecki (*Hypnotist*), Daniel Webb (*American*)
Feature 35 mm colour 107 mins

1988
Siedm Dni w Tygodniu (Seven Days a Week)
Director: Krzysztof Kieślowski
Cinematography: Jacek Petrycki
Editor: Dorota Warduszkiewicz
Sound: Michał Żarnecki
Production Company: City Life, Rotterdam
Documentary 35 mm colour 18 mins

Krótki Film o Zabijaniu (A Short Film about Killing)
Director: Krzysztof Kieślowski
Screenplay: Krzysztof Kieślowski, Krzysztof Piesiewicz
Cinematography: Sławomir Idziak
Editor: Ewa Smal
Sound: Małgorzata Jaworska
Music: Zbigniew Preisner
Production Company: Tor and Polish Television
Cast: Mirosław Baka (*Jacek*), Krzystof Globisz (*Piotr*), Jan Tesarz (*Taxi-driver*), Zbigniew Zapasiewicz (*Police inspector*), Barbara Dziekan-Wajda (*Cashier*)
Feature   35 mm colour   85 mins

Krótki Film o Miłości (A Short Film about Love)
Director: Krzysztof Kieślowski
Screenplay: Krzysztof Kieślowski, Krzysztof Piesiewicz
Cinematography: Witold Adamek
Editor: Ewa Smal
Sound: Nikodem Wołk-Łaniewski
Music: Zbigniew Preisner
Production Company: Tor
Cast: Grażyna Szapołowska (*Magda*), Olaf Lubaszenko (*Tomek*), Stefania Iwińska (*Godmother*), Artur Barciś (*Young man*), Stanisław Gawlik (*Postman*), Piotr Machalica (*Roman*), Rafał Imbro (*Bearded man*), Jan Piechociński (*Blond man*)
Feature   35 mm colour   87 mins

Dekalog (The Decalogue)
Ten television drama films

Dekalog 1 (Decalogue 1)
Director: Krzysztof Kieślowski
Screenplay: Krzysztof Kieślowski, Krzysztof Piesiewicz
Cinematography: Wiesław Zdort
Editor: Ewa Smal
Sound: Małgorzata Jaworska
Music: Zbigniew Preisner
Production Company: Polish Television
Cast: Henryk Baranowski (*Krzysztof*), Wojciech Klata (*Paweł*), Maja Komorowska (*Irena*), Artur Barciś (*Man in the sheepskin*), Maria Gładkowska (*Girl*), Ewa Kania (*Ewa Jezierska*), Aleksandra Kisielewska (*Woman*), Aleksandra Majsiuk (*Ola*), Magda Sroga-Mikołajczyk (*Journalist*)
35 mm colour   53 mins

Dekalog 2 (Decalogue 2)
Director: Krzysztof Kieślowski
Screenplay: Krzysztof Kieślowski, Krzysztof Piesiewicz
Cinematography: Edward Kłosiński
Editor: Ewa Smal
Sound: Małgorzata Jaworska
Music: Zbigniew Preisner
Production Company: Polish Television
Cast: Krystyna Janda (*Dorota*), Aleksander Bardini (*Consultant*), Olgierd
Łukaszewicz (*Andrzej*), Artur Barciś (*Young man*)
35 mm colour   57 mins

Dekalog 3 (Decalogue 3)
Director: Krzysztof Kieślowski
Screenplay: Krzysztof Kieślowski, Krzysztof Piesiewicz
Cinematography: Piotr Sobociński
Editor: Ewa Smal
Sound: Nikodem Wołk-Łaniewski
Music: Zbigniew Preisner
Production Company: Polish Television
Cast: Daniel Olbrychski (*Janusz*), Maria Pakulnis (*Ewa*), Joanna Szczep-
kowska (*Janusz's wife*), Artur Barciś (*Tram-driver*)
35 mm colour   56 mins

Dekalog 4 (Decalogue 4)
Director: Krzysztof Kieślowski
Screenplay: Krzysztof Kieślowski, Krzysztof Piesiewicz
Cinematography: Krzysztof Pakulski
Editor: Ewa Smal
Sound: Małgorzata Jaworska
Music: Zbigniew Preisner
Production Company: Polish Television
Cast: Adrianna Biedrzyńska (*Anka*), Janusz Gajos (*Michal*), Artur Barciś
(*Young man*), Adam Hanuszkiewicz (*Professor*), Jan Tesarz (*Taxi-driver*),
Andrzej Blumenfeld (*Michal's friend*), Tomasz Kozłowicz (*Jarek*), Elżbieta
Kilarska (*Jarek's mother*), Helena Norowicz (*Doctor*)
35 mm colour   55 mins

Dekalog 5 (Decalogue 5)
Television version of *A Short Film about Killing*
35 mm colour   57 mins

Dekalog 6 (Decalogue 6)
Television version of *A Short Film about Love*
35 mm colour   58 mins

Dekalog 7 (Decalogue 7)
Director: Krzysztof Kieślowski
Screenplay: Krzysztof Kieślowski, Krzysztof Piesiewicz
Cinematography: Dariusz Kuc
Editor: Ewa Smal
Sound: Nikodem Wołk-Łaniewski
Music: Zbigniew Preisner
Production Company: Polish Television
Cast: Anna Polony (*Ewa*), Maja Barełkowska (*Majka*), Władysław Kowalski (*Stefan*), Bogusław Linda (*Wojtek*), Bożena Dykiel (*Ticket woman*), Katarzyna Piwowarczyk (*Ania*)
35 mm colour   55 mins

Dekalog 8 (Decalogue 8)
Director: Krzysztof Kieślowski
Screenplay: Krzysztof Kieślowski, Krzysztof Piesiewicz
Cinematography: Andrzej Jaroszewicz
Editor: Ewa Smal
Sound: Wiesława Dembinska
Music: Zbigniew Preisner
Production Company: Polish Television
Cast: Maria Kościałkowska (*Zofia*), Teresa Marczewska (*Elzbieta*), Artur Barciś (*Young man*), Tadeusz Łomnicki (*Tailor*)
35 mm colour   55 mins

Dekalog 9 (Decalogue 9)
Director: Krzysztof Kieślowski
Screenplay: Krzysztof Kieślowski, Krzysztof Piesiewicz
Cinematography: Piotr Sobociński
Editor: Ewa Smal
Sound: Nikodem Wołk-Łaniewski
Music: Zbigniew Preisner
Production Company: Polish Television
Cast: Ewa Błaszczyk (*Hanka*), Piotr Machalica (*Roman*), Artur Barciś (*Young man*), Jan Jankowski (*Mariusz*), Jolanta Piętek-Górecka (*Ola*), Katarzyna Piwowarczyk (*Ania*), Jerzy Trela (*Mikolaj*)
35 mm colour   58 mins

Dekalog 10 (Decalogue 10)
Director: Krzysztof Kieślowski
Screenplay: Krzysztof Kieślowski, Krzysztof Piesiewicz
Cinematography: Jacek Bławut
Editor: Ewa Smal
Sound: Nikodem Wołk-Łaniewski
Music: Zbigniew Preisner
Production Company: Polish Television
Cast: Jerzy Stuhr *(Jerzy)*, Zbigniew Zamachowski *(Artur)*, Henryk Bista *(Shopkeeper)*, Olaf Lubaszenko *(Tomek)*, Maciej Stuhr *(Piotrek)*
35 mm colour   57 mins

1991
La Double Vie de Véronique (Podwójne Życie Weroniki)
Director: Krzysztof Kieślowski
Screenplay: Krzysztof Kieślowski, Krzysztof Piesiewicz
Cinematography: Sławomir Idziak
Editor: Jacques Witta
Art Director: Patrice Mercier
Music: Zbigniew Preisner
Executive Producer: Bernard-P. Guireman
Producer: Leonardo de la Fuente
Production Company: Sidéral Productions/Tor Production/Le Studio Canal Plus
Cast: Irène Jacob *(Weronika/Véronique)*, Aleksander Bardini *(Orchestra conductor)*, Władysław Kowalski *(Weronika's father)*, Halina Gryglaszewska *(Weronika's aunt)*, Kalina Jędrusik *(Gaudy woman)*, Philippe Volter *(Alexandre)*, Sandrine Dumas *(Catherine)*, Louis Ducreux *(Professor)*, Claude Duneton *(Véronique's father)*, Lorraine Evanoff *(Claude)*, Guillaume de Tonquedec *(Serge)*, Gilles Gaston-Dreyfus *(Jean-Pierre)*
35 mm colour   98 mins

1993
Trois Couleurs: Bleu
Director: Krzysztof Kieślowski
Screenplay: Krzysztof Kieślowski, Krzysztof Piesiewicz
Cinematography: Sławomir Idziak
Editor: Jacques Witta
Art Director: Claude Lenoir
Sound: Jean-Claude Laureux
Sound Mixer: William Flageollet
Music: Zbigniew Preisner

Executive Producer: Yvon Crenn
Producer: Marin Karmitz
Production Companies: MK2 SA/CED Productions/France 3 Cinéma/ CAB Productions/Tor Production
Cast: Juliette Binoche (*Julie*), Benoît Régent (*Olivier*), Florence Pernel (*Sandrine*), Charlotte Véry (*Lucille*), Hélène Vincent (*Journalist*), Philippe Volter (*Estate agent*), Hugues Quester (*Patrice*), Emmanuelle Riva (*Mother*), Florence Vignon (*Copyist*), Jacek Ostaszewski (*Flautist*), Yann Tregouet (*Antoine*)
35 mm colour   98 mins

Trois Couleurs: Blanc
Director: Krzysztof Kieślowski
Screenplay: Krzysztof Kieślowski, Krzysztof Piesiewicz
Cinematography: Edward Kłosiński
Editor: Urszula Lesiak
Art Directors: Halina Dobrowolska, Claude Lenoir
Sound: Jean-Claude Laureux
Sound Mixer: William Flageollet
Music: Zbigniew Preisner
Executive Producer: Yvon Crenn
Producer: Marin Karmitz
Production Companies: MK2 SA/France 3 Cinéma/CAB Productions/Tor Production
Cast: Zbigniew Zamachowski (*Karol Karol*), Julie Delpy (*Dominique Vidal*), Janusz Gajos (*Mikołaj*), Jerzy Stuhr (*Jurek*), Grzegorz Warchoł (*Elegant man*), Jerzy Nowak (*Old peasant*), Aleksander Bardini (*Lawyer*), Cezary Harasimowicz (*Inspector*), Jerzy Trela (*Monsieur Bronek*), Cezary Pazura (*Bureau de change proprietor*), Michel Lisowski (*Interpreter*), Piotr Machalica (*Tall man*), Barbara Dziekan (*Cashier*), Marzena Trybała (*Mariott employee*), Philippe Morier Genoud (*Judge*), Francis Coffinet (*Bank employee*), Yannick Evely (*Metro employee*), Jacques Disses (*Dominique's lawyer*), Teresa Budzisz Krzyżanowska (*Madame Jadwiga*)
35 mm colour   92 mins

Trois Couleurs: Rouge
Director: Krzysztof Kieślowski
Screenplay: Krzysztof Kieślowski, Krzysztof Piesiewicz
Cinematography: Piotr Sobociński
Editor: Jacques Witta
Art Director: Claude Lenoir
Sound: Jean-Claude Laureux
Sound Mixer: William Flageollet

Music: Zbigniew Preisner
Executive Producer: Yvon Crenn
Producer: Marin Karmitz
Production Companies: MK2 SA/France 3 Cinéma/CAB Productions/Tor Production
Cast: Irène Jacob (*Valentine Dussaut*), Jean-Louis Trintignant (*Judge Joseph Kern*), Frédérique Feder (*Karin*), Jean-Pierre Lorit (*Auguste Bruner*), Samuel Lebihan (*Photographer*), Marion Stalens (*Veterinary surgeon*), Teco Celio (*Barman*), Bernard Escalon (*Record dealer*), Jean Schlegel (*Neighbour*), Elżbieta Jasinska (*Woman*), Paul Vermeulen (*Karin's friend*), Jean-Marie Daunas (*Theatre manager*), Roland Carey (*Drug dealer*)
35 mm colour   99 mins

BIBLIOGRAPHY

AMIEL, VINCENT, 'Plongées dans la passion: *Trois Couleurs: Bleu, Blanc, Rouge*', *Positif* 403 (Sept. 1994), 24–5.

—— *Kieślowski* (Paris: Rivages/Cinéma, 1995).

—— 'Vous ne savez pas, en France, ce qu'il en coûte de vivre dans un monde sans représentation', *Positif* 409 (Mar. 1995), 58–60.

—— 'Kieślowski et la méfiance du visible', *Positif* 423 (May 1996), 73–4.

ANDREW, GEOFF, *The 'Three Colours' Trilogy* (London: BFI, 1998).

ARBAUDIE, MARIE-CLAIRE, 'Leonardo de la Fuente: "Une législation inadéquate"', *Film français* 2373 (25 Oct. 1991), 6.

AUMONT, JACQUES, *L'Œil interminable* (Paris: Séguier, 1995).

BANGH, LLOYD, *Imaging the Divine: Jesus and Christ-Figures in Film* (Kansas City: Sheed and Ward, 1997).

BARTHES, ROLAND, *La Chambre claire* (Paris: Gallimard, 1980).

BAZIN, ANDRÉ, *Qu'est-ce que le cinéma?* (Paris: Editions du Cerf, 1975).

BEAUVOIR, SIMONE DE, *Brigitte Bardot and the Lolita Syndrome* (London: André Deutsch, 1960).

BÉNOLIEL, BERNARD, 'Krzysztof Kieślowski: souvenirs de Pologne', *Cahiers du cinéma* 515 (July/Aug. 1997), 9.

BERGSON, HENRI, *Matière et mémoire* (Paris: Presses Universitaires de France, 1939).

BOLESŁAW, MICHAŁEK, and TURAJ, FRANK, *The Modern Cinema of Poland* (Bloomington and Indianapolis: Indiana University Press, 1988).

BOUNDAS, CONSTANTIN V., and OLKOWSKI, DOROTHEA (eds.), *Gilles Deleuze and the Theater of Philosophy* (New York and London: Routledge, 1994).

BREN, FRANK, *World Cinema 1: Poland* (London: Flicks Books, 1986).

BRENEZ, NICOLE, 'Cinématographie du figurable', in Jean-Luc Godard, *Le Mépris, L'Avant-scène cinéma* 412/413 (May/June 1992), 1–9.

BUTLER, JUDITH, *Gender Trouble: Feminism and the Subversion of Identity* (New York and London: Routledge, 1990).

—— 'Imitation and Gender Insubordination', in *Inside/Out: Lesbian Theories, Gay Theories*, ed. Diana Fuss (New York and London: Routledge, 1991), 13–31.

—— *Bodies that Matter: On the Discursive Limits of Sex* (New York and London: Routledge, 1993).

CAMPAN, VÉRONIQUE, *Dix Brèves Histoires d'image* (Paris: Presses de la Sorbonne nouvelle, coll. 'L'Œil vivant', 1993).

CARUTH, CATHY, *Unclaimed Experience: Trauma, Narrative, and History* (Baltimore: Johns Hopkins University Press, 1996).

—— (ed.), *Trauma: Explorations in Memory* (Baltimore: Johns Hopkins University Press, 1995).

CAVENDISH, PHIL, 'Kieślowski's Decalogue', *Sight and Sound* 59/3 (Summer 1990), 62–5.

CIMENT, MICHEL, and NIOGRET, HUBERT, 'De Weronika à Véronique', interview with Krzysztof Kieślowski, *Positif* 364 (June 1991), 26–31.

CIMENT, MICHEL, and AMIEL, VINCENT, 'Entretien avec Krzysztof Kieślowski: "La fraternité existe dès que l'on est prêt à écouter l'autre"', *Positif* 403 (Sept. 1994), 26–32.

CLOVER, CAROL, *Men, Women and Chainsaws: Gender in the Modern Horror Film* (London: BFI Publishing, 1992).

COATES, PAUL, *The Story of the Lost Reflection: The Alienation of the Image in Western and Polish Cinema* (London: Verso, 1985).

—— 'Exile and Identity: Kieślowski and his contemporaries', in *Before the Wall Came Down: Soviet and East European Filmmakers Working in the West*, ed. G. Petrie and R. Dwyer (Lanham, MD, and London: University Press of America, 1990), 103–14.

—— 'Metaphysical Love in Two Films by Krzysztof Kieślowski', *The Polish Review* 37/3 (1992), 335–43.

—— 'The Sense of an Ending: Reflections on Kieślowski's Trilogy', *Film Quarterly* 50/2 (Winter 1996–7), 19–26.

—— (ed.), *Lucid Dreams: The Films of Krzysztof Kieślowski* (Trowbridge: Flicks Books, 1999).

CROSS, FRANK LESLIE, *The Oxford Dictionary of the Christian Church* (Oxford: Oxford University Press, 1983).

DELEUZE, GILLES, *Cinéma 1: L'Image-mouvement* (Paris: Minuit, 1983).

—— *Cinéma 2: L'Image-temps* (Paris: Minuit, 1985).

—— and GUATTARI, FÉLIX, *L'Anti-Œdipe: Capitalisme et schizophrénie* (Paris: Minuit, 1972).

—— and PARNET, CLAIRE, *Dialogues* (Paris: Flammarion, 1996).

DOBSON, JULIA, 'Nationality, Authenticity, Reflexivity: Kieślowski's *Three Colours: Blue* (1993), *White* (1993) and *Red* (1994)' in *French Cinema in the 1990s: Continuity and Difference*, ed. Phil Powrie (Oxford: Oxford University Press, 1999), 234–45.

DOUIN, JEAN-LUC, *Wajda* (Paris: Editions Cana, 1981).

DUNKLEY, CHRISTOPHER, 'Rules for Life, Polish Style', *Financial Times* (13 June 1990), 17.

DYER, RICHARD, *White* (London: Routledge, 1997).

ESTÈVE, MICHEL (ed.), *Krzysztof Kieślowski* (Paris: Lettres Modernes/Etudes Cinématographiques, 1994).

FELMAN, SHOSHANA, and LAUB, DORI, *Testimony: Crises of Witnessing in Literature, Psychoanalysis, and History* (New York and London: Routledge, 1992).

FREUD, SIGMUND, 'Creative Writers and Daydreaming' [1908], *Penguin Freud Library 14: Art and Literature* (Harmondsworth: Penguin, 1985), 129–41.

—— 'The "Uncanny"' [1919], *Penguin Freud Library 14: Art and Literature* (Harmondsworth: Penguin, 1985), 335–76.

—— 'Beyond the Pleasure Principle' [1920], *Penguin Freud Library 11: On Metapsychology* (Harmondsworth: Penguin, 1991), 269–338.

—— 'Moses and Monotheism' [1939], *Penguin Freud Library 13: The Origins of Religion* (Harmondsworth: Penguin, 1990), 237–86.

FUSS, DIANA, *Essentially Speaking: Feminism, Nature and Difference* (New York and London: Routledge, 1989).

—— *Identification Papers* (New York and London: Routledge, 1995).

—— (ed.), *Inside/Out: Lesbian Theories, Gay Theories* (New York and London: Routledge, 1991).

GARBOWSKI, CHRISTOPHER, 'Krzysztof Kieślowski's *Decalogue*: Presenting Religious Topics on Television', *The Polish Review* 37/3 (1992), 327–34.

—— *Krzysztof Kieślowski's Decalogue Series: The Problem of the Protagonists and their Self-Transcendance* (Boulder, CO: East European Monographs, 1996).

GODARD, JEAN-LUC, *Le Mépris*, *L'Avant-scène cinéma* 412/413 (May/June 1992).

GROSZ, ELIZABETH, 'Deleuze, Bergson and Uncharted Futures: Duration, the Virtual and History' [as yet unpublished paper].

INSDORF, ANNETTE, 'Cinematic Poetry: An Affectionate Look at Krzysztof Kieślowski's *Three Colours: White*', *Film Comment* 33/2 (Mar./Apr. 1997), 46–9.

—— *Double Lives, Second Chances: The Cinema of Krzysztof Kieślowski* (New York: Miramax Books, 1999).

JOUSSE, THIERRY, 'D comme Deleuze', *Cahiers du cinéma* 497 (Dec. 1995), 26–7.

KAFKA, FRANZ, *The Transformation and Other Stories*, trans. Malcolm Pasley (Harmondsworth: Penguin, 1992).

KAŁUŻYŃSKI, ZYGMUNT, 'Technology shakes Culture: Cinema is dying, Cinema is blooming', *Polityka* 10 (8 Mar. 1997), 50–3. [In Polish.]

KEHR, DAVE, 'To Save the World: Kieślowski's Three Colours Trilogy', *Film Comment* 30/6 (Nov.–Dec. 1994), 10–20.

KEMP, PHILIP, '*Trois Couleurs: Rouge*', *Sight and Sound* 4/11 (Nov. 1994), 54–5.

KIEŚLOWSKI, KRZYSZTOF, 'Je doute, je doute toujours' (interview), *Télérama hors-série* (Sept. 1993), 90–6.

—— 'La dramaturgie du réel', *Positif* 409 (Mar. 1995), 56–7.

—— 'Ma vie est tout ce que je possède', *Positif* 423 (May 1996), 75–6.

—— and PIESIEWICZ, KRZYSZTOF, *Decalogue: The Ten Commandments* (London: Faber and Faber, 1991).

—— —— *Trois Couleurs* (Paris: Arte Editions/Hachette, 1997).

KIM, JOHN, 'Poles Apart 1: Krzysztof Kieślowski', *Columbia Film View* 10/1 (1992), 2–5, 39.

KISSEN, EVA H., '*The Double Life of Véronique*', *Films in Review* 43/5–6 (May/June 1992), 195–6.

KLIMA, IVAN, *My First Loves*, trans. Ewald Osers (Harmondsworth: Penguin, 1986).

MACCABE, COLIN, review of *Le Mépris*, *Sight and Sound* 6/9 (Sept. 1996), 55–6.

MACNAB, GEOFFREY, '*Trois Couleurs: Bleu*', *Sight and Sound* 3/11 (Nov. 1993), 54–5.

—— 'The World in a Drop of Water', *The Independent* (25 July 1996), section 2, 8–9.

MALCOLM, DEREK, 'Human touch of a master', *The Guardian* (14 Mar. 1996), 15.

MASSON, ALAIN, 'Subjectivité et singularité: *La Double Vie de Véronique*', *Positif* 364 (June 1991), 24–5.

—— '*Trois Couleurs: Rouge*: La naïveté du manipulateur', *Positif* 403 (Sept. 1994), 21–3.

METZ, CHRISTIAN, *Psychoanalysis and Cinema: The Imaginary Signifier* (London: Macmillan, 1982).

MULVEY, LAURA, 'Visual Pleasure and Narrative Cinema', in *Feminism and Film Theory*, ed. Constance Penley (London: BFI, 1988), 57–68.

—— *Fetishism and Curiosity* (London: BFI, 1996).

MURAT, PIERRE, '1,2,3, Kieślowski', *Télérama* 2475 (18 June 1997), 32–4.

NARBONI, JEAN, 'Gilles Deleuze... une aile de papillon', *Cahiers du cinéma* 497 (Dec. 1995), 22–5.

ORR, JOHN, *Cinema and Modernity* (Cambridge: Polity, 1993).

PECK, AGNÈS, '*Trois Couleurs Bleu/Blanc/Rouge*: Une trilogie européenne', in *Krzysztof Kieślowski*, ed. M. Estève (Paris: Lettres Modernes/Etudes Cinématographiques, 1994), 147–62.

PERNOD, PASCAL, 'L'amour des personnages (*Brève Histoire d'amour*)', *Positif* 346 (Dec. 1989), 26–7.

PETRIE, GRAHAM, and DWYER, RUTH (eds.), *Before the Wall Came Down: Soviet and East European Filmmakers Working in the West* (Lanham, MD, and London: University Press of America, 1990).

PIZZELLO, STEPHEN, 'Piotr Sobociński: *Red*', *American Cinematographer* 76/6 (June 1995), 68–74.

PORTNOY, SEAN, 'Unmasking Sound: Music and Representation in *The Shout* and *Blue*', *The Spectator* 17/2 (Spring/Summer 1997), 50–9.

PROUST, MARCEL, *A la recherche du temps perdu*, I (Paris: Gallimard, 1954).

PULLEINE, TIM, '*A Short Film About Love*', *Monthly Film Bulletin* 57/676 (May 1990), 131–2.

PYM, JIM, '*A Short Film About Killing*', *Monthly Film Bulletin* 56/671 (December 1989), 371–2.

PYNOOS, ROBERT S. (ed.), *Posttraumatic Stress Disorder: A Clinical Review* (Lutherville, MD: Sidran Press, 1994).

RAGLAND, ELLIE, and WRIGHT, ELIZABETH, 'The Double Life of Véronique: An Enquiry into the Existence of Woman', *Australian Journal of Psychotherapy* 14/1–2 (1995), 13–19.

RAYNS, TONY, 'Kieślowski crossing over', *Sight and Sound* 1/11 (Mar. 1992), 22–3.

—— 'Glowing in the Dark', *Sight and Sound* 4/6 (June 1994), 8–10.

ROBINSON, EMMA, 'Memory, Nostalgia and the Cinematic Postmodern', unpublished paper read at the 1996 *Screen* Studies Conference.

RODOWICK, D. N., *The Difficulty of Difference* (New York: Routledge, 1991).

—— *Gilles Deleuze's Time Machine* (Durham, NC, and London: Duke University Press, 1997).

ROMNEY, JONATHAN, '*The Double Life of Véronique*', *Sight and Sound* 1/11 (Mar. 1992), 42–3.

ROPARS-WUILLEUMIER, MARIE-CLAIRE, 'The Cinema, Reader of Gilles Deleuze', in *Gilles Deleuze and the Theater of Philosophy*, ed. C. V. Boundas and D. Olkowski (New York and London: Routledge, 1994), 255–61.

RUPPERT, PETER, '*The Double Life of Véronique*', *Cinéaste* 19/2–3 (Dec. 1992), 63–5.

SALECI, RENATA, and ŽIŽEK, SLAVOJ (eds.), *Gaze and Voice as Love Objects* (Durham, NC, and London: Duke University Press, 1996).

SAUVAGET, DANIEL, '*La Double Vie de Véronique*', *La Revue du cinéma/Image et son* 473 (July/Aug. 1991), 47.

SHIPMAN, DAVID, 'Obituary: Krzysztof Kieślowski', *The Independent* (14 Mar. 1996), 16.

'A Short Film about *Decalogue*: An interview with Krzysztof Kieślowski', transcript (London: Black & White Productions, 1995).

STOK, DANUSIA (ed.), *Kieślowski on Kieślowski* (London: Faber, 1993).

STRICK, PHILIP, '*No End*', *Monthly Film Bulletin* 55/650 (Mar. 1988), 76–7.

SZYMBORSKA, WISŁAWA, *View with a Grain of Sand* (London: Faber and Faber, 1996).

Télérama, *Le Décalogue de Krzysztof Kieślowski* (1989).

Télérama hors série (Sept. 1993), *La passion Kieślowski*.

TOBIN, YANN, *et al.*, 'Décalogue: la preuve par dix', *Positif* 351 (May 1990), 31–41.

TOUBIANA, SERGE, 'Le Cinéma est deleuzien', *Cahiers du cinéma* 497 (Dec. 1995).

TURIM, MAUREEN, *Flashbacks in Film: Memory and History* (New York and London: Routledge, 1989).

VINCENDEAU, GINETTE, 'Juliette Binoche: From Gamine to Femme Fatale', *Sight and Sound* 3/12 (Dec. 1993), 22–4.

—— *The Companion to French Cinema* (London: Cassell, 1996).

WILLIAMS, LINDA, *Viewing Positions: Ways of Seeing Film* (New Brunswick, NJ: Rutgers University Press, 1995).

WILSON, EMMA, 'Re-viewing Desire: Love and Death in Hiroshima', *La Chouette* 26 (1995), 18–25.

—— *Sexuality and the Reading Encounter: Identity and Desire in Proust, Duras, Tournier and Cixous* (Oxford: Clarendon Press, 1996).

—— '*Three Colours: Blue*: Kieślowski, Colour and the Postmodern Subject', *Screen* 39/4 (Winter 1998), 349–62.

WYATT, JUSTIN, 'Sight and Sound A–Z of Cinema: M Marketing', *Sight and Sound* 7/6 (June 1997), 38–41.

ŽIŽEK, SLAVOJ, *Looking Awry: An Introduction to Jacques Lacan through Popular Culture* (Cambridge, MA: MIT Press, 1991).

—— 'No Sexual Relationship', in *Gaze and Voice as Love Objects*, ed. R. Saleci and S. Žižek (Durham, NC, and London: Duke University Press, 1996), 208–49.

INDEX

SOCIETY FOR FRENCH STUDIES

The Society for French Studies, the oldest and leading learned association for French studies in the UK and Ireland, exists to promote teaching and research in French studies in higher education. The Society's activities include:

• Editing the *French Studies* quarterly journal and its companion *French Studies Bulletin*

• Editing the catalogues of research projects, *Current Research in French Studies* and *Postgraduate Research*—now online at www.sfs.ac.uk

• Hosting an annual conference with distinguished guest speakers and a variety of workshops across the spectrum of French studies

• Maintaining a website with rapidly expanding resources for those working in French Studies (**www.sfs.ac.uk**)

• Supporting research through:

› Conference and seminar grants for events in the UK and Ireland

› The R. H. Gapper annual prizes for scholarship at undergraduate, postgraduate, and book-publication levels

› Subsidising publication of *Legenda* Research Monographs in French Studies

› Grants for postgraduate travel to the SFS annual conference, and reduced postgraduate conference and membership fees

› Extension of the postgraduate membership rate to new lecturers in their first three years of employment

Membership enquiries: Dr Gill Rye
Institute of Germanic and Romance Studies, University of London
Senate House, Malet Street, London WC1E 7HU, UK
membership@sfs.ac.uk

The Society for French Studies is charity no. 1078038 and is a company, limited by guarantee, registered in England and Wales, no. 3801778, whose registered office is the Taylor Institution, Oxford OX1 3NA.